Life Behind

the Potted Plant

By: Miz M

*for
Bill & Jean*

*Doris Michael
1999*

Gabbard Publications

Published by:
Gabbard Publications
1829 Grubb Road
Lenoir City, TN 37771

Copyright 1998 by D. M. G. Michael
Printed In USA
1st Printing

ISBN: 0-9622608-6-X

NOTICE: The information, illustrations and historical
accounts contained in this book are true and accurate to
the best of our knowledge. The author and publisher
disclaim all liability incurred in connection with the use
of the information contained in this work. However,
should an error in historical accuracy appear, it is solely
the responsibility of the author and publisher and will be
corrected in later editions of this book.

Cover photos from family archives.
Cover design and layout by Alex Gabbard.
Book design and layout by Alex Gabbard

Acknowledgements:

People who answered questions and provided information for this book must be given credit. Many thanks to Linda Hamlin of the Dobson Library, Ken Badgett, Ray Martin, Lora Martin, Bernice Dockery Hyatt, Kay Speas Alley, Julie Axsom Barber and probably many more people to whom I must apologize for being overlooked in ascribing proper credit.

At this point I lay my pen down with a sigh of relief. Alex nudged, prodded and kept me at it. Michaela provided many insights and recollections where mine have become foggy with age. Her photograph albums have proven invaluable, and going through many of the photos contained herein has given me the opportunity to reflect on the lives and times of my family that must seem ancient to everyone else.

This is a simple telling of an old woman's memories. Eighty is a good age to reflect and recall. Who knows, maybe someone in generations hence will find this work illuminating of my family, perhaps their family, that would remain lost without committing these stories and photos to print.

Doris Michael

Little Richmond, North Carolina
Summer, 1998

Dedicated
to
My Children

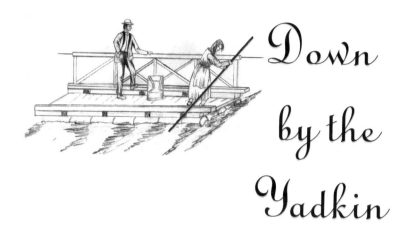

Down by the Yadkin

The ferry bell clanged its demand for service, then repeated its summons before Lily could strip the bread dough from her hands.

"Drat!" she said, "and not a man on the place!" Lily knew that strangers didn't like to be kept waiting. So for a big girl, she covered the ground quickly and presented

1

herself with dispatch... a ferry maid with pink cheeks, panting from her downhill run.

And a stranger he was. Muscled shoulders supported a backpack of impressive bulk. With his face turned up river toward the opposite riverbank, he wasted no time on greetings.

"That the Mitchell bridge?"

"Yessir... to carry the railroad coming up the old Indian trail. 'Twill connect Greensboro, Salem and Wilkesboro."

His quick turn betrayed surprise at hearing a female voice; eyes flashed interest.

"You the ferryman?" Whimsy rode a pleasant grin.

"How much to the north bank?"

"Two pence."

Pedestrian fare was handed and accepted. Lily gave half her attention to poling her flat craft, mostly a push from down-river to prevent current drift. The greater half was turned on her passenger. Young men - handsome and well-spoken - traveling alone raised questions.

Bump! They had arrived at the landing. Stepping to sandy footing, the traveler examined bridge building activity just above the confluence of the Mitchell River and the Yadkin. He was not aware that a dam shut in Mitchell water to power a mill little more than a slingshot cast above the railroad bridge-in-progress. Several wagons waited in the shade by the roadway, teams patiently swishing their flywhisk tails. The day was just right for enjoying the cool breeze, and no one seemed in a hurry.

"Where could I find the bridge-builder?"queried the new arrival.

"In the mill house, gettin' dinner. 'Bout this time

2

every day. You a bridge hand?"

"Nope. United States mail will come on the train.
Passengers and Freight Station will go up by a siding just
before the bridge on this side. Mail will be my business.
Every day, up and down trains'll be passing through here."

Eyes wide, Lily considered this marvel. Never had
she had a question answered so civilly - women were
beneath men's dignity on such important matters. As she
tucked her chin and took a firm grip on her pole, he looked
straight at her and stuck out his hand.

"My name is Burch."

Buster did his best thinking while doing the Bread
Run - Mom's name for a trip to the mill. The mule had only
one speed; carrying boy and wheat sacks in a leisurely sway
that required no guidance; and both boy and beast were
enjoying a holiday.

After a while the surefooted mule began descending
the ridge that fell away toward a creek well up stream from
the mill. Buster was thinking that he would finally get to *see*
the new railroad bridge that he'd heard so much fuss about,
but he had been warned not to waste time playing around.
Mom saw to it that he shouldn't dally.

"Shucks," he muttered. "Ain't nobody goin' to
know if I cross it just once."

There was no more delightful sound to Buster than
echoes of the mule's plodding along as it crossed the Snow

Creek Bridge. That bridge was just a spittin' span compared to the Mitchell, and each hoof beat resonated between the concrete uprights that amplified the sound.

Chunk, whap... Chunk, whap... Chunk, whap.

Buster wondered if the much larger bridge being built across the Mitchell would echo like the one crossing Snow Creek.

Once across the bridge he followed the riverside path downstream, crossing one small branch before reaching the mill. Water in the river pooled calmly into a wide shallow that grew deeper and deeper as he neared the mill. Overhanging birch and sweetgum limbs swaying in the gentle breeze, birds twittering all around, and the sweet smells of the woods was a tempting invitation to take a dip, but that warning not to waste time "playing" tumbled over and over in his mind. Mom knew that a boy like him and a river pool were hard to keep separate, especially if a good swingin' vine happened to be among the trees.

Noise of rushing water grew louder the nearer he got to the mill. River water calm and pooled behind heavy planking of the dam was diverted into a sluice that carried a run of it to power an overshot wheel. With its hefty uprights and base struts supporting the angled dam, each slick with moisture and water moss, the dam was a great place to play, but not today.

Instead, the sound of the mill filled Buster's senses. He breathed deeply, his chest expanding to contain all the fragrances of the forest and river spray. A deep hum underlay the rumble-swish-clatter of mill magic that converted grain into flour, corn to meal, and the thought of bread fresh-baked in his mother's oven - it all started here, and he could just taste her hot biscuits and butter.

Sliding off the mule onto the mill-porch, he was met by Gee, the miller, who unloaded the "grindings" to a rickety wheeled contraption that Buster was certain had to be older than dirt. It was just the thing he could fix up, but not before he got to that new bridge.

"Tie your beast in the shade, Buster," the miller advised. "It'll be a spell, but there's the bridge to see. Lots of goings-on over there. Just don't fall off the thing." The miller hoisted a sack of grain to his shoulder and disappeared into the dusty clatter of his calling, and Buster wasted no time in setting off for the bridge.

It was a first for the boy. Hefty metal framework rising from massive concrete pillars that grew right out of the river seemed impossible. But there it was, and he imagined men pointing and shouting all over it. He wished that he had been able to watch them build it. He could see how the hefty I-beams were fixed in place with round headed fasteners that held it together like a giant steel web of triangles. The clatter of hammers on the steel had faded away, but the smell of freshly creosoted ties underlying the rails was pungent. It wouldn't be long before the first steam engine would be huffing and puffing its way across the bridge, and he didn't want to miss that show for sure.

Buster crept to the brink of the trestle and looked down at the water below. The miller's comment about not falling off showed itself to be good advice as the dimpled, clear water running over a rocky bed was certain to be a hard landing. Just below the bridge the water divided around a small island formed by ancient Mitchell deposits thrown up from inside the caissons used to form freshly poured concrete into pillars to support the trestle.

The mouth of the Mitchell just a few dozen yards

away emptied into the Yadkin River's muddy murk in swirls of clean water swallowed up by the red tide. The mix of the two rivers meant the end of the Mitchell and its beginnings from the watershed of the Blue Ridge Mountains to the north only a few dozen miles away.

"Oh boy!" Buster mused to himself. Nobody to keep him away made the bridge even more inviting. He stepped from crosstie to crosstie carefully because a slip between them could mean a broken leg, or worse. Each step took his concentration until he discovered that he was squarely over the river. He peered between the ties at the water below; its motion and the height of his perch made his head begin swimming. With nothing to grasp for support, he suddenly felt an emptiness in the pit of his stomach. Instinctively, he sat down on one of the rails and closed his eyes. The hot, sun-heated rail against his hand and buttocks caused a quick move, and he landed in sticky little pools of creosote that stuck to his skin and pants. At the moment his wooziness overcame the dread of what his mother was going to say about that, and in a minute or two he got his senses back just as a voice penetrated his consciousness. He looked back to see a man waving his arms at him to get off the bridge.

Buster inched back to solid ground and stood to face a jawing, but it was a friendly face atop a small, wiry body that confronted him. With his hand out as if to greet a grown man, he announced, "Howell Carter, bridge builder and construction fack-toe-tum," then vigorously pumped the boy's hand, only to notice afterward that he now had a spot on his hand that matched Buster's.

"Yessir... I'm Buster."

"Like my bridge, hey?"

6

"Yeah... Sir. But I ain't never seen nothin' like this before. It's all metal, 'cept for the ties. Steel I reckon. What holds it together?" he queried, pointing back at the structure. "Them's not nails."

It was evident that Buster had asked the right question, and the next twenty minutes were filled with explanation, and more explanation. The builder loved his work, and a kindred spirit had been discovered in an inquisitive boy who suddenly became enamored with bridge building.

"Come back next week, my boy. I'll be gone but my bridge will stand ready to carry the iron horse," invited Carter.

Buster would not forget.

Burch Station

T he word was out. Bright shiny rails were ready; the bridge was finished, and the train was coming.

Buster fidgeted with excitement as he waited beside the wagon - as usual his mother was last out the door.

Everybody was going to Burch Station to see the train.

"Hurry, hurry, Mama! It'll be gone before we get there," implored her son.

But Mama was certain that the event would be later than expected. Talk would be called for at every stop all up the line from Greensboro, and "Big Men" would be riding...

to inspect the track and how it rode.

Mama was right. All the hat lifting and hand shaking along the way made the Southern's arrival in Burch Station later than anyone, especially Buster, ever imagined. But it was an event not to be missed, a big event for Little Richmond, so no one left before the blowing of a distant whistle fired the gathered crowd with excitement. Buster jumped up into the wagon to see better, and with all eyes in the crowd fixed toward the track way off in the distance, the gabble petered out as expectations changed to held breaths.

Buster, now standing in the driver's seat, was first to see it. "There she comes," he yelled, pointing down the tracks toward Crutchfield. That cloud of steam and smoke rising from the trees meant only one thing; then from the narrow split among the trees there it was, the prettiest thing he'd every seen. The silver nose of the green engine and tender all polished to sparkles would be the talk of Little Richmond for years to come. Belching its huff in majestic splendor, whistle blowing its approach, but rolling far too slowly for Buster, the Southern Limited arrived in Burch Station to start a new era: a regular schedule of fares.

The "Up" train: 15¢ fare to Elkin

9

Little Richmond was now connected with the rest of the world.

More hat lifting and hand shaking followed as one "Big Man" after another got off and said whatever they said, but Buster couldn't keep his eyes off that engine. Like a great dragon harnessed to the rails, it lay there steaming, huffing, its giant wheels just waiting to be turned loose. He walked around and around it, then following the invitation of the fireman, he climbed up into the engineer's cabin. It was all wonderfully magical to him, and sooner than he hoped the engineer climbed up and an "All Aboard" signal was given. The whistle blew, and away pulled the Limited. Buster climbed up on the wagon and stood on the seat to catch the last glimpse of its smoke billowing up through the trestle up line in the distance. All the way home, that gleaming engine was all he talked about.

Where did the railroad come from? And where did it go? Buster saved up his questions for a meeting with Mr. Carter - a man who loved to talk.

"Yep, yep; after the Civil War, the railroad started west outta Greensboro. Cape Fear and Yadkin Valley Railroad. Came along to link Virginia with Mt. Airy. Didn't happen; convict labor graded the railroad bed, some in leg irons, all in stripes. Too much mountain!" Mr. Carter gestured.

"Mt. Airy Railroad joined with the Richmond and Danville Railroad along the Yadkin all the way to Wilkesboro. Then the whole railroad was leased to Southern in 1894, for ninety-nine years, and took one name; Norfolk Southern."

Buster didn't know that he would live to see a remnant of that line change to a short line operating from

Rural Hall up to Roaring River. For now, though, the big steamer coming up from Greensboro was the biggest thing that had ever happened, so far as he knew, and he wasn't going to miss any of it.

Handbills told of coming events for Burch Station: a station house with two waiting rooms and a freight depot; a Section Foreman's house nearby; a resident ticket agent. People were all astir with the new developments. All kinds of workers would be needed to cut timber and haul it to H. Carter's new sawmill. Carpenters, too. And that's not all.

Some said, "You just wait and see; the road will get moved." And it was. A new route through Little Richmond was staked out. Where the old road went straight toward the Mitchell River, the new road veered left down the ridge winding its way toward Burch Station to run along the Yadkin and on to a new crossing beyond it at the Mitchell River. There would be another bridge built, a new one for the new highway that was certain to go in between the railroad span and the mill. Burch Station brought big things to this area.

Unlike the old road bed that was awash in mud whenever it rained, the new road was wider and improved by state crews. And later it was hard surfaced.

Times were a-changing. That old road had seen its day, and it made no difference that General Sherman and his bluecoats marched along it for seven days and nights. All that was forgotten.

New growth generated new ambition. Or maybe it's the other way around. Anyway, talk of the goings-on at Burch Station, the new highway, new bridges was on everyone's lips, and heads nodded wisely at the prospects. The very idea of jobs, good paying jobs that would sure beat working the tobacco fields and sawmills sparked a renaissance in Little Richmond. Buster figured that he would be promoted to Wagoner; before long he'd be driving his own team with a load of timber to be ripped up into planking for all the building that was sure to take hold of the community.

Time passed, and Buster found a sweetheart in Jonesville. Her family attended services at the Pentecostal Holiness church across the narrow street from Jonesville School as did his. Now driving a big lumber truck, Buster found a few stolen minutes to court Martha. When he brought her home to a new house, she could truthfully say that her man sawed out every piece of it.

"He started with the trees," she'd say. But Martha had another tale to tell. "It was Christmas time, and we went to a program at Jonesville School. There was a good crowd in the auditorium on the second floor, and a big iron stove sat in the middle.. And that's where the floor SPLIT! Stove, people, benches - everything fell through.

"It was a terrific MESS. The Garris boy was burned badly; he was next to the stove and *everything* fell on top of him! But nobody was killed. Dr. Salmons went three days without sleep tending to all the folks."

Buster was glad the school didn't catch fire. "It was a pure TRAP," he said. "They were all night getting people out."

Some of the old timers got their heads together and reckoned that Carter and Burch were partners because both were newcomers, and both of them had money in their pockets. That was made clear to everyone when they both bought land; Burch got hold of several acres, and built a new house, a two-story with broad porches front and back, plenty of windows, and lots of rooms. It went up beside the old road across from the Wallace house, and if that wasn't enough, he built a huge barn on the opposite side. Not only that, he got a crew together to dig a well for his house and another one for the barn. The man must have had big plans.

Now why would anybody need a big house like that with an even bigger barn? More head nodding put together the idea that Burch was building a hotel and his barn was really a livery. Time soon proved the idea, and then people were saying that Vance Burch was putting Little Richmond on the map.

It wasn't long after Vance came to this part of the country that he got to courting Lily, and no one doubted that she would have him. And, sure enough, they made themselves into a business partnership; Lily "took lodgers" in the house, and Vance started a livery service out of his big barn. With steady money coming in, they did good for themselves and prospered. Vance drove the mail buggy to meet the train, took on the mail bags, and delivered them to the tiny post office in the Wallace house.

Somebody named the new Fourth Class post office, Rusk. Don't know why. Sort of the same for Little Richmond. Don't know where it got its name, either. Or why Martinboro got changed to Jonesville.

From the post office, the mailman and horse did the Star Route six days a week while Lily raised the boys and fed the travelers on the long table over which she presided. When the boys grew older, Vance built a store right on the road over near the barn, angled sort of from the east side of the house. Burch's store carried general merchandise (the sign said so), and right off it was manned by the oldest of their four boys.

Well, you guessed it; the storekeeper soon got married. Another house went up for his help mate, and help she did. It was another fine house with a wide porch that circled all around the front, situated a short walk from the back of the store.

With all the work to do there was no time for idle hands in the Burch family. When house and store were quiet, the new Mrs. Burch put her treadle Singer to work stitching together shirts and dresses and all sorts of things like that.

Now, this part of the country was known to have a spirit-making industry hidden here and there along creeks, and one among us called "A" was known to often be "under the weather" following an over-indulgence with his corn squeezin's.

By the time that Burch Station, the new highway, Rusk Post Office, and the big houses that Little Richmond became known for had been around a while, it had been a long time since Lily had poled the ferry across the Yadkin. Times were changing, and like the mill on the Mitchell, the ferry wasn't used much any more. When it was washed

14

away in the flood of 1916, no one was motivated to reinstate the service because the new road and its bridge served an increasingly motorized public.

Sometime around then the dam washed through and the mill burned, leaving nothing but its concrete foundation. Before long, the winding, 2-lane Route 268 had been around long enough that the old road and General Sherman were little more than stories told on rainy days. With no trace of the ferry, the road that once led to it across the Yadkin valley bottomland was reclaimed by the farmers. And when the new bridge on Route 601 went in across the river down at Crutchfield, the ferry faded from memory.

The Kaiser War took away the strength of Little Richmond. All the young men were drafted to serve their country in that first World War. Things were quiet around here and a few tears fell to the earth that had sustained each family. Then during the final year of the war a deadly influenza swept the military, and it soon took its toll on civilians, too. Little Richmond buried more of its people.

To make things worse, the winter of 1918 was the longest and coldest anybody could remember. The Yadkin River, Ol' Muddy, froze solid. Ice was so thick that a car dealer in Elkin drove a Buick out on it.

That was the year I was born, christened Doris Anthea Martin. That old road I spoke of went straight westerly in front of the house that my father, John Winston Martin, and my mother, Alice Lora Martin, came to live in during 1913.

Little Richmond

In 1900 the village of Little Richmond lay along a wagon track through North Carolina's Surry County that connected the county seat of Rockford (later moved to Dobson) and the town of Elkin. Across the Yadkin River from Elkin, on the Yadkin County side, Martinboro lay. A covered bridge connected the two. Later, Martinboro was renamed Jonesville, the name it still carries.

The Vance Burch house was actually two structures joined with an "L" shaped porch that faced a well house behind the house. Further from the well, his large stable housed livestock and several rigs; buggies and wagons were for hire.

Another well served the livery stable and the store.

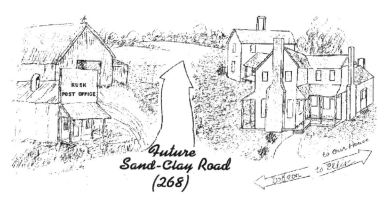

Vance Burch hotel, store and stable, Little Richmond c. 1910

Both man and beast could be fed and bedded; travelers came to the Burch house by road and rail as it was only a mile or two along the new road down hill to Burch Station.

Following the Civil War a new faith called Missionary Baptist was preached along the river. On a ridge near the junction of the Dobson-to-Crutchfield road, now called Route 601, and the spur to the river that went through Little Richmond, now called Route 268, an itinerant preacher organized the Mt. Hermon Church beside what became known as the Mt. Hermon Church Road. A church was built along with a cemetery installed on the opposite side of the road.

Enthusiasm was fueled by a wave of "joiners." Soon, a group in Little Richmond organized and built a church on a knoll along the old road that passed by the Martin house just past the barn. Again, the graveyard was on the opposite side of the road. A settlement including the Burch "hotel," store, church, and school spread down the ridge toward Snow Creek bridge and the Mitchell River.

Growing demand for a more direct link between the

17

railway station and county seat resulted in construction of a sand-clay road that split the Burch property. The "hotel," as many people called it, now stood within the branches of the "Y" formed by the new and old roads. Lily had to cross the new road to get to her garden, barn and cow pasture, and the Martin house ended up on a road no longer used.

Because the new road moved away, the Little Richmond church became isolated, and wise heads nodded that they really should move the church. So, move it was, to the opposite side of the new road about a mile toward Twin Oaks from the Burch "hotel." And true to form, the cemetery was on the opposite side of the road. But the move meant that the old cemetery was forgotten. Its slate headstones without names on them were left to grow into a clump of trees in the edge of a pasture.

Further up the new road on the other side, on the next hill, a two-room school house was built. When coming toward the Burch "hotel" from Twin Oaks, the school stood on one hill on the right, the church on the next hill on the left, and both faced the new sand clay road that went between their front steps.

Gasoline powered automobiles began to become more common by the Twenties, and the multitude of jokes about mud holes and frequent tire blowouts underlay the need for more improvements. The community of Little Richmond needed a hard surfaced road.

About this time, road building became a state function rather than a haphazard county matter. There was talk among politicians trying to gather up votes for their stay in the Governor's mansion that the state of North Carolina really ought to get its citizens out of the mud. So, hard surface roads became the rallying call that would get the sand clay road capped with asphalt some years later. A good many of the sand clay road's crooks and turns were straightened, and a few concessions had to be made along pasture fences and fields to allow for widening and straightening before the State assumed control and gave it a highway number. But rounding the hills and drops had to follow what God gave the road builders, and even with their best intentions, North Carolina State Route 268 quickly became known as the crookedest road in the county. Its meander from Burch Station to Elkin followed along the north side of the Yadkin River, and it just as quickly became known as the "River Road."

Gradually, as people got into the habit of driving cars, an entire string of little country stores sprang up along Route 268. You couldn't go more than a few miles before coming to this store and its gas pump on that side, or that store and its gas pump on this side. It didn't take long before someone figured out that two gas pumps sitting out away from the store allowed for two cars to drive up for gasoline, one on either side of the pumps rather than only one car that could be gassed up from the single pump fixed near the store.

And with the cars came commuting to work. Elkin offered jobs at the Chatham Blankets mill and furniture factories, along with the stores that lined Main Street, so the daily drive by car to a regular paying job meant that most of the little country stores along Route 268 were bypassed.

Mostly locals frequented the stores, and as people became more comfortable with "goin' to town," traffic on Route 268 grew and grew and went right by the stores. After a while, one by one, they closed. Most of the buildings have survived, but they either sat empty and derelict or became a church of who knows what denomination.

During the early days of cars in our part of the county, doctors and salesmen were the first to tackle the elements in them, and braving creeks without bridges, then mud made bottomless by spiraling wheels needed the solution that farmers knew well: a team of mules often solved the plight of trapped motorists.

Just after the turn of the century, young John Winston Martin had been clerking his brothers' store up at Salem Fork. It was located in the Big Woods where the families of his three older brothers, Newton, Richard, and Tom, settled and carved out farms. When John decided to enter the world of mercantilism for himself, he brokered a freight car load of fertilizer from a siding at Burch Station. By night he boarded with Lily and enjoyed her cooking. By day he sold fertilizer from the siding. Farmers rolled their wagons up to the doors of his freight car, and with exchange of the necessary funds, off they went to work their fields while John counted his money.

By the time that his fertilizer was sold, John's earnings meant that he could travel a bit, and like most young men, he wanted to see the world first hand. He headed for Texas. The day came that he waved farewell to Lily and boarded the coal burning steamer that left Burch Station for Winston-Salem and all points south.

By then John had spent enough time in Little Richmond that he had come to know the community and its people pretty well. Tucked away in his memory were the fine houses that spoke of this community's prosperity. Its Rusk Post Office, Burch Station, Burch "hotel," school, and church, all connected by the sand clay road traveled by more and more cars, would figure in his life again. He would return, but for reasons he could not have imagined.

He would always remember the high point of his long journey to Texas and often told of crossing the Mississippi. Although the muddy Yadkin might have seemed a formidable obstacle to John, the similarly muddy Mississippi presented impossible proportions. It was far too wide for a bridge, and he was convinced that there wasn't likely to ever be one across that stretch of water.

But there was a ferry. It was fitted with rails locked into the yard of land tracks so that the engine could roll four cars on, uncouple them, run along a switch to a parallel track and pick up more cars. It was a show for the passengers who were not allowed to leave their coaches. The whole process was reversed on the opposite riverbank and led on to Texas.

After visiting with relatives and learning of Texas and its cowboy and Indian lore, John decided to head back east. He had seen an advertisement from the new R. J. Reynolds Tobacco Company that was looking for a representative to go into Kentucky and introduce two products; shredded tobacco in small, drawstring bags (cigarette papers sold separately) for the roll-your-own smoker, and

21

chewing tobacco in twists or slabs, the latter with the sweet aroma of licorice.

John signed on. With his new order book and sample case, he braved the unknown. Easy travel ended when he stepped down from the train into Union Station behind the Phoenix Hotel in Lexington, Kentucky. There he leased a horse-drawn hack with driver from a livery and set out for places and experiences he would never forget.

Later in life when yarning about this trip, he stressed two conditions; he was always lost and always cold. Upon winding up at Maysville on the Ohio River, when he turned in his order book his traveling in distant places was over; thereafter he stayed within his own state, first selling shoes (a bout with typhoid fever ended that enterprise), tobacco, then wholesale groceries and a missed opportunity; for $50 his friend John Lowe offered him partnership as half of what became the huge Lowe's enterprise.

When John found a refined city-bred wife in East Bend, a series of unexpected events caused him to return to Little Richmond. There he would buy the house I was born in, their first child. The house was built in 1900. Today their granddaughter, my first child, lives in it.

The Martin saga as I know it is from Mayo to the Big Woods. "If at first you don't succeed, try, try again" must have been Richard Martin's motto. He grew up in Rockingham County on the Mayo River and married Elizabeth Ayres - but was soon widowed with a young son. Richard found another mother for young Hunter Pleasant Martin in Elisabeth Morgan - but again he was soon widowed with two more children.

Elizabeth Kellam Smith, herself widowed with seven children, was the third Elizabeth for Richard. They moved to Dobson and added four more Martins to their family. The three sons, William Richard, John Winston and Spencer served the Confederate cause during the war of Northern Aggression, then returned to civilian life afterward; William, now a colonel, became a guard in the penal system; Spencer became a judge; and John Winston went into the hotel business and married a daughter of Thomas Hamlin, Aradella. They were my Grandparents.

John and "Dell" made a home in the Martin Hotel that faced the west side of the County Courthouse in Dobson. It was home for both their family and for the traveling public. He served as Register of Deeds, as many records show; we treasure one of his handwritten marriage licenses from 1873. But his health broke, and they removed to a log home beside the Hamlin Ford on Fisher River, hoping for a recovery that never came. When he died, eldest son Newton became the man of the family, helping raise Thomas, Richard, (who acquired the nickname Coot), Elizabeth, and John Winston, born posthumously.

Farming for themselves and for others became the brothers' way of life. At twelve, John was tending tobacco barns through nights of curing that required spliting wood

23

for the fires used to cure the leaves. Yet he was well schooled in reading and writing. Arithmetic and business skills were later sharpened when he tended store while his older brothers farmed.

As they accumulated a second start in a new location westward of the Fisher River, a place known as Salem Fork, they acquired land and built a house, then planned for a store and set into motion changes to one room of their house that was soon stocked with goods that people all around came to rely upon. That enterprise soon grew into a fine store building constructed at the intersection of the east-west road from Dobson-to-Mountain Park and the connecting road to Twin Oaks that junctioned with Route 268. Southward on this highway came Little Richmond, Rusk, and Burch Station. The brothers' new store faced northward and had a high front with wide glass windows on either side of a large door set back into the front and up from the ground a few steps.

The entire store was built on short, stocky pilings so that any accumulated rain water would have to get a couple of feet above the ground to reach inside floor level. If that happened, since Salem Fork was on high ground, the sur-roundings would have needed an ark to combat the deluge.

For a turn-of-the-century store way out in the country, Martin Brother's store was a sight to behold. It was built of clapboard siding, long with a high roof sloped toward the back where a loading dock allowed transfer of fertilizer and other bulky materials without going through the front door. Inside, on the right from the entrance, was a long counter, divided about mid-way, with jars and cans and display cases for about anything that could be imagined.

On the wall behind it from floor to ceiling stood all

manner of shelves and pigeon holes for bottles and tins and
similar things, more of what could be imagined, and on the
left wall of the store was another floor-to-ceiling array of
cupboard doors, shelves and pigeon holes set full of boxes
and cloth and bolts and hardware and almost everything to
meet any and every need.

John was the first storekeeper. He tended the store
several years and carefully kept ledgers that tell of life in

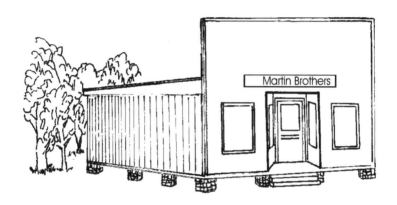

←to Dobson   to Mountain Park→
Martin Brothers Store, Salem Fork, 1920 - 1980

Salem Fork. In his ledgers, one column for the date is
followed by the item transacted, then by whom followed by
details of the exchange, for most everything was bartered.
Little money actually changed hands.

In this manner of business, a picture of how things
like chickens were exchanged for hinges and how they
became valued according to John Martin and the person
needing something from the store's stock evolved. Those
hand written ledgers remain keepsakes of the family.

25

To the west of the store lay the Big Woods, and in the edge of it about a mile toward Mountain Park the brothers founded the Salem Fork Christian Church.

Many years hence, John Winston Martin, my father, was to be the last founding father to step with cane in hand along the aisles of the church. Having played the church piano since I was twelve, since 1930, I played "Don't Fence Me In," his favorite song, along with hymns fitting of the occasion when he was rolled from the podium to be laid to rest with his brothers and family after a long and full life. The founders of Salem Fork who had carved out life in the Big Woods had all passed away.

The church, the store, Newton's fine Victorian house across the road, and Tom's substantial but less imposing house on the same side of the road as the store but through a stretch of woods - and facing the same direction as the store - had been the focus of Salem Fork for decades.

All but the church are gone now; tax assessments spelled destruction of the work of many lives. The store exists only in memories among the old folks now, and a motel sits on the ground where Grandma Dell, Newt, and all of us laughed and lunched on Sundays.

Newt and Tom took over the store operation in 1909, and John began his travels as a sales representative for the Wright Shoe Company, then Reynolds Tobacco, and then Tomlinson Wholesale Groceries out of North Wilkesboro.

By then, Martin's Store was known far and wide as a real department store with shoes, china, toiletries, housewares, personal goods, and groceries among a much longer list. Along with successful farming, the brothers had made their mark as merchants.

The "big house," Newton's, was never to hear the sounds of his own children, as he had none. And late in life when he finally married old maid school teacher Kizzie Bray, she made herself less well received than she might have.

In the meantime, John had offered his new wife a life in the Big Woods, but the cabin he labored to build was snubbed as much too rough hewn, and he located with his new wife closer to civilization in Little Richmond, rather far in those days from his brothers.

For a while, the good years you might say, Grandma Dell had all her sons and their families nearby, and with her pride in their accomplishments, she departed the "big house" in 1929 satisfied with her life's work. With its electric lights from a Delco battery system and indoor bath with running water, *they* had done it with love and elbow

The Martin brothers home stood from 1924 to 1984. A motel stands on this location now. Grandma Dell, Newton and Tom with his family, Bessie and their six children, made this Salem Fork's finest home. When Newt married Kizzie Bray, both beyond child being age, Tom built another home for his family and moved down the road a piece. The "old folks" had this fine house all to themselves. In its demise, it was disassembled for reuse as salvage material.

grease.

John's only son, Ben Hamlin Martin, was my youngest sibling with sister Lucille between us. The sons of Richard, who was always as "Coot," carried the family name for another generation. Coot's boys, Bill and Tom, with two and three sons, respectively, keep Martin a viable surname in Salem Fork and Surry County for their generation. Tom and his wife, Bessie, had a large family of mostly girls with Ray about the same age as Ben. They were great friends. Ray followed Newt's example and had no family.

All but John's family were in the Salem Fork area. From Little Richmond, Ben grew from his boyhood of being doted over by two older sisters to become a sailor in the US Navy during World War-2, then settled with his beautiful wife, Sadie Draughn of Dobson, in High Point.

These words rest in my own recollections, the stories told to me by Grandma Dell, and records from several sources. My drawings here and there where a photo hasn't been found help to illustrate the lives and times as I recall them.

Ray, Grandma Dell, Joyce and Aunt Bessie on the sidewalk in front of the Newton and Tom Martin home, Salem Fork c. 1930

Mud & Dust

The Twenties brought a wave of up-lifting as ambition pulled North Carolina onward and upward. And along with our neighbor counties, road construction and school building changed the face of Surry County.

Little Richmond was chosen for a seven-grade school to be housed in a fine brick building. A large auditorium filled with tilt-bottom seats affixed to the floor faced a stage on the north end and classrooms surrounded it on three sides. Two front doors invited our children in for miles around. They were on either side of the first grade room and led into the building with a straight shot along the open sides of the auditorium to the doors of the other classrooms to the right or left, depending on which door you came in. Then, straight on out the back where the restrooms were tacked onto the building some years later when a new wave

Little Richmond School c. 1927 stood for about 50 years. Two generations of us children, including me, schooled, sang, and danced here. It was the focus of our community. I taught 4th grade, my own children, too.

School floor plan:
- 5th grade
- stage
- 4th grade
- 6th grade
- 3rd grade
- 7th grade
- 2nd grade
- Office
- 1st grade
- Supplies

TEACHER'S CONTRACT

STATE OF NORTH CAROLINA, } ARTICLES OF AGREEMENT
_____ County.)

THIS AGREEMENT Entered into between the Public School Committee of _Little Richmond_ District, _Marsh_ Township, _White_ Race, on the _____ day of _July_, 192_, in accordance with Sections 101, 130, and 158-171 inclusive, which are hereby made a part of this contract, and _Eula C. Poston_ _Lakeland Florida_ a Teacher holding a _Grammar Grade B_ Certificate, No._____, which expires _____, 192_, Witnesseth:

That said teacher agrees to teach a Public School in said district for the current school term, said school to begin on the _3d_ day of _October_, 192_7_, to discharge faithfully all the duties imposed on teachers by the Public School Law of North Carolina, and to give at least 30 days notice to the County Superintendent before terminating this contract, and in consideration thereof said committee promises to pay the said teacher the sum of ($ _____) _____ Dollars for each month said teacher shall teach.

This contract is not valid until approved and signed by the County Superintendent of Public Instruction, nor for more money than accrues to the credit of the district for the fiscal year during which the contract is made.

This contract is null and void if the teacher does not hold certificate of class and number indicated above.

(Signed) _____, Chairman.
Approved _____ _____, Secretary.
County Superintendent. _Eula C. Poston_, Teacher.

A COPY OF THIS CONTRACT MUST BE KEPT ON FILE IN THE OFFICE OF THE COUNTY BOARD OF EDUCATION. A COPY RETAINED BY THE COMMITTEE. AND A COPY PLACED IN THE HANDS OF THE TEACHER.
(Teachers are urged to read sections 158-171 of the School Law, which define the duties of teachers in public schools.)

Daddy was Secretary of the School Board for Little Richmond School. He hired Eula Poston as one of the first teachers. She boarded at our house. Over a half century later, Eula became the second Mrs. John W. Martin and returned to the house.

31

of improvements brought electricity and plumbing.

As each child rose from grade to grade, their classroom simply moved around the building. From the First Grade in the front of the building came the Second Grade, the first room along the easterly side of the building. The Third Grade room came next, then the Fourth and Fifth that I would come to know well. The big day came when the student crossed the auditorium to the westerly side and progressed through the grades from front of the building to the rear. Later on, what had been the Eighth Grade room was converted to a lunch room, and up front was the principal's office and a little store offering candy and snacks.

Above the auditorium the ceiling rose higher with a row of windows all around that let in additional light, and just a little ahead of center hung a rope to the bell. Its clanging was the duty of the janitor, who, at the prescribed time, rang out to all who could hear that it was time to go to school. Many students around the country knew schools like Little Richmond, they were here and there.

From the day the Little Richmond School opened to the day it closed, it only had one janitor. He lived just down the westerly path toward the graveyard on the Joe Layne's Mill road that cut through in front of his house.

That dirt road turned off to the right from the sand clay road just about at the new church and wound its way through the countryside to the Layne's mill on Snow Creek and beyond toward Salem Ford and Mountain Park.

Large families were the rule back then. Instead of tiny neighborhood schools that had sprinkled the Appalachians before, the State took hold of education, and one large consolidated facility brought all our children together from miles around. Yellow school buses traversed each road, and for the high school pupils, a bus went on from Little Richmond to Dobson, then returned each day to retrace its route depositing children where they had gotten on early that morning.

Each school day burst alive with the din, chatter, and laughter of elementary school children who arrived with the first bus. They had to wait until the other buses arrived before classes began, so they had time to sprinkle the morning with excited giggles and playful antics. Classes didn't take up until all the children had arrived, sometimes taking forty-five minutes or so, occasionally longer if the weather was bad, and the auditorium filled with mischievous boys and prim girls.

This was a country school, and a finer one wasn't to be found anywhere. Its red bricks accented with white trim, its broad roof rising to the bell tower, and flagpole out front sat among trees in a rather picturesque setting. Each room with a wall full of tall windows and a door to the outside was to serve three generations of Little Richmond families. Our children, mine too, passed through its doors and sat through day after day of "learning" as we teachers opened their minds to the world and helped them become responsible adults with, I believe, a firm grasp of what was important and a will to achieve.

The Little Richmond School was to become part of me when I began teaching, and after seeing the faces of so many children wanting to learn, asking questions, and being so proud of their grades, a part of me died along with the school when it closed, was boarded up and became derelict, then was torn down some years ago. I was not alone. Little Richmond lost one of its landmarks that everyone around here knew well. It was a part of each of us.

From its very beginning, a wave of social doings provided ways of meeting and greeting; Fiddlers Conventions, box suppers, plays, lectures too - for improvement was in the air; ice cream suppers, singings, and contests! These were all part of the life of our Little Richmond School. And did we ever hand out prizes, prizes of all kinds: the best speller; the prettiest dress for whatever the occasion or season might be; most popular boy or girl, which tended to show who was making eyes at whom; the King and Queen of the day; the ugliest outfit let the boys show off just how grungy they could look and get by with it. And dances. We always had music, if I can permit myself a pat on the back here, because my teaching went far beyond textbooks and assignments to the music I loved. My old upright pump organ had its place by the stage, until it was damaged and broken by someone, but for years and years it provided the musical background for our children who sang and danced in shows and plays that were performed throughout the school season.

And there was "learning"- plenty of it. It was during this time that Magic Lantern slides taught everyone about the world in pictures and such things as germs, and small bars of Palmolive soap were given to pupils who proudly showed their washed hands for gold stars.

Back then, girls covered every inch of themselves when working outside because a lady was white and willing to swelter under bonnet and long sleeves for beauty's sake.

When dressing for social mingling, ruffles, flounces, sashes, bows, and ribbons were the order of the day - but no cosmetics. Ladies didn't paint. Rice powder, maybe, or pink Tangee on the lips to "prevent chapping," but no such thing as lipstick. Times did change, though, and shorter skirts and rolled hose were shocking to the elders of our community when they became standard attire.

And the old folks blamed automobiles for taking young people out of supervisory range. One mother said, "As long as my girls stayed CLOSE, I knowed what went on; but when they got AWAY, they got 'dulterated!"

So it was in Little Richmond as it was, I'm sure, throughout the rest of the country.

Those days were ruled by mud and dust. The dust wasn't too bad, unless you got caught in a summer whirlwind, but the mud clung to everything. But come planting time and mud was what everyone wanted. Rows through tobacco fields were laid off in such a way as to capture any rain runoff, so after every storm, rain collected between the rows and made long troughs of muddy water; muddier when we got into them.

Planting tobacco wasn't looked upon with much favor, but with the mud came playful slipping and sliding, stomping and splashing that made the work more fun and helped it go faster.

If the ground was wet, the process was to "peg" the young tobacco sprouts into muddy rows. Your peg was a tapered stick that was forced into the wet ground and wobbled around to open the mud suitably for a plant. Then a foot stomped next to it closed the earth around the young plant, and before long a field full of sprouts a couple of feet or so apart were in the ground where their roots took hold and grew into tall plants with broad leaves that would go to market in the fall and wintertime. But market came only after a season of working the fields six days a week, then the curing, then the grading and tying that seemed to go on endlessly. Come Christmas, it was all done, and the next three months were devoted to school.

Bare feet were just the thing for "pegging" tobacco, six days a week in the spring, except for stepping on a rock, sharp horsenettles or maybe cuckleburrs. As the tobacco grew and summer dry set in, weeds between the rows and plants had to be cleared, and hoeing in the sun was the norm. As the summer progressed, prickly things on the ground didn't bother toughened feet because going without shoes was normal summertime attire for boys and girls alike.

Mud was an ever-present pedestrian problem, though, so one dressed up - or should I say down - as far as the feet, and carried "good shoes" in hand until arrival at the chosen destination where they were changed. Oftentimes, a row of muddy brogans rested under a doorstep, or at church they'd line a back wall.

John & Alice

Young John Martin toted his sample case into the impressive store of W. A. Martin (no relation) in East Bend and met his future wife. She wore a sunbonnet and was minding store while her Papa ate lunch. They spoke the necessary....

"Would like to show the proprietor a line of shoes." Miss Alice, as he would come to learn her name, mentioned that Mr. Martin would be back from lunch in a little while.

John was now on the road selling for the Augustus P. Wright Shoe Company. After selling tobacco products for R. J. Reynolds, including their new Prince Albert tobacco in bright red "tins" with hinged, flip open tops, he had chosen to travel closer to home. He was a handsome man, tall, slender and strong enough to easily handle the large trunks of shoe samples, especially if he was showing off a bit for a

Mama's Daddy owned this store; W. A. Martin & Co. General
Merchandise, East Bend, North Carolina c. 1890. He also
owned a tobacco bag factory (below).

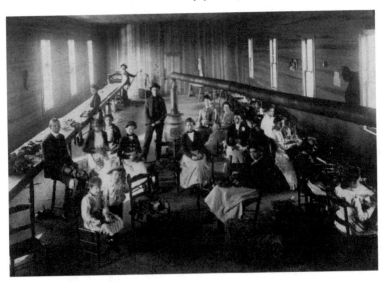

pretty lady.

Mr. W. A. lived in the big white house on the corner lot across the street. He sold dry goods in the upper floor of his store, and Miss Alice told John, "You can look over our stock, if you would like to."

Her manner of speaking told that she was a refined and cultured lady. In fact she was "finished" having received such "finishing" at a school for young women, Salem Academy in Old Salem.

John inspected the half-floor above the general merchandise, and liked what he saw both there and below. Soon the owner returned, and they exchanged greetings. Mr. W. A. introduced him to Alice Martin, his daughter.

It wasn't proper to ask questions of such a fine lady, but just a flash of eyes was enough for John to decide that he was interested in this Alice Martin. These developments take time, but a start had been made.

Courting was hampered by distance; John would drive his rig to Crutchfield where the horses were left with Haywood Barker while the train conveyed him easterly to the siding at Donnaha. The mail carrier finished his journey by taking him as a passenger into East Bend. John asked if he could write to her, and when Alice accepted, an exchange of corres- pondence for some time helped them get better acquainted, along with some surprises.

In one of her letters, Alice mentioned that he might not want to continue writing, she was a widow, the youngest in East Bend, and that she had a child that had also passed away. Her honesty was accepeted; John had found the love of his life. He always called her his sweetheart. Their romance blossomed and a date was set.

John and Alice were wed, and he set for himself the task of building their new home in the Big Woods at Salem Fork where his brothers had set down roots. His plan was to join them, but Miss Alice wasn't happy with the isolation and farm life that they presented. With the help of his brothers, the Martin boys built a sizable cabin of logs near a creek. It was a start, sure to grow into something bigger and nicer in time, but it was in the wrong direction for a refined city girl. Proud of his handiwork and pleased to have built their home, John sat down on a log beside his new wife and asked if she could be happy here. She didn't answer; her tears told the whole story.

John remembered Little Richmond. There were those fine houses and a growing community fed by the traffic of both the sand clay road and the Southern Railroad at Burch Station. Salem Fork was, after all, well removed from any culture and was dominated by forests all around. It was miles and miles from any town, Dobson being the closest, and except for his brothers and their families, the area offered little more than a lifetime of hard work in a backwoods setting.

It was 1913 when John and Alice set up housekeeping in the almost new house built on the old road to Elkin a half-mile or so past the Burch "hotel". The lay of the land was a knoll that rolled off gently from both the back of the house and the front of the house that sat on a ridge that led west from it to the Mitchell River. No one seems to know when this road was built; it had been in use since before the Civil War, perhaps long before that.

40

John Winston Martin and Alice Lora Martin c. 1910, my father and mother. Although of the same last name, John and Alice were from different lines of the Martin family name.

So, this large home built in 1900 with its towering hardwoods, mulberry trees on the west side and a line of cherry trees sat on the main thoroughfare leading east from the Mitchell. When the sand clay road went in, the world curved in a direction away from the Martin place and headed toward Burch Station.

Although its high hip roof suggested that the house might be a two-story, it was really just one level with a cellar entered from its own doorway at the rear of the house. High ceilings and tall windows in its six large rooms helped control summer heat. Three rooms lay on either side of a huge hallway that led from the front door to the back door opposite it. The front door was at the left end of an "L" shaped wrap-around porch along the front and right side of the house while the back door led onto a screened-in

41

back porch. Several concrete steps led from this porch and its spring maintained screen door and aimed directly at the well and windlass that pulled up buckets full of clear, fresh water.

Then, on to the barn with its high hay loft, mule stalls and corn cribs in the central portion, a hay shed to the right and a row of milking stalls on the left that was connected to passage to the pasture through a pole gate.

Just beyond this barn was the location of the first Little Richmond Church, and across the "lane," as the old road to the Mitchell River became known, quietly lay the community's first cemetery in its ignored over-growth.

The house, barn and pastures behind it and along the "lane" became known as the Martin Place. It was the nucleus of added acres through the years. Sixty-eight years later when this generation was laid to rest, the original holding of land had grown to one hundred, sixty-eight acres as adjacent land came on the market. Some land that could have expanded the Martin Place wasn't added on the judgment of John Martin.

Along the Mitchell River was rough and tumble ground overgrown with all sorts of thickets, briars, and such. When that land came available, John decided against it saying riverbank land wasn't good for anything. Years later that very same property was highly valued as places where people could go to get back to nature. It's still pretty rough.

John continued as a sales representative in an area that included most of Surry and Wilkes Counties to the west and Yadkin County to the south. It took him two weeks to make the circuit; on Saturdays he turned in orders at North Wilkesboro, did the records, and picked up payroll money for the chair factory in Ronda, which he delivered on his way home.

And Alice became his farmer. The work that woman did! One cow became two, then more; in ten years sixteen milkers were pastured around the place. Tobacco and corn were grown by tenants, all needing her to manage from time to time, and John had taken on a new duty that came to live with them.

Little Richmond had a new 8-room school house, and its very first teacher, a young and pretty Eula Poston from south Georgia, boarded at the Martin Place. With everything else to do, boarding school teachers more than filled the Martin house. Soon there were children, and Miss Alice swung it all.

Big gardens produced lots of food - fresh in season and canned for other times of the year. She kept herself busy with early morning and evening milking, gardening in the morning, canning in the afternoon, and there were meals to prepare, sometimes with with hungry farm hands to

Mama, 1909, in mourning, having lost both her infant son and her husband that year.

serve, then clean up before evening sewing and bedtime. And then came birthing the children, three of us, then keeping after us once we could get around for ourselves. Everything in the Martin household kept her days more than

43

occupied.

Miss Alice had the first pressure cooker anybody had heard of around Little Richmond, and she used it. Demonstration clubs were the newest thing for homemakers, and county agents organized clubs for women where they were taught the latest techniques in cookery, stitchery, and general housewifery. Alice was a faithful club member all her active years.

In those days, bread and meat were produced at home; beef and pork were grown and butchered, sausage ground and canned, smoke houses were stocked with hanging hams and shoulders, and side meat lay salted down.

The big oval table in the Martin dining room was always full: family, live-in help, teachers, and boarders; they all pulled up chairs for many meals over the years. This table and its glass-backed buffet were a gift from Mr. Cox to his new wife, Alice Martin. He had cut down a large walnut tree and had it fashioned into a fine table that could be expanded with inserts. The matching buffet housed dining room finery in its drawers, inside its cabinet doors, and on top. It was to serve three generations and is in daily use to this day in the home of a Martin grandson.

A fireplace in the front room backed up to a similar fireplace in the dining room, and a big wood-burner range kept the kitchen warm around the clock. Hot water didn't just happen; first it was lifted cold from the well, then carried in buckets up the steps to a big copper boiler that was never allowed to go dry. Hot water was a luxury doled out by Miss Alice's careful hand.

Yet, with all the work, there was free time to sit on shady porches, to visit, to read, and occasionally Mr. Martin strummed and plucked out tunes on his banjo. Rarely did you see people in a hurry; that was yet to come. Women always had a bit of sewing or knitting in hand while talk went on; bean shelling and corn shucking went more easily with several hands participating and with tongues wagging.

Year 'round, the Martin house was a beehive of activity. People coming and going, always more work than could be done in a day's time that somehow managed to get done. Alice kept everything going while John was on the road. With us children, Gramma Flora, Gramma Dell, school teachers, farm hands in and out, we all did just fine in her care.

Mama firmly believed that idle hands were the Devil's workshop. With all the work that kept her busy, she still managed to turn out beautifully crocheted doilies and trim on table cloths and the like. Sunday was her day to rest, and rest she did.

Our Folks

Our part of the country had its colorful characters. They came with the times, I suppose; some who just couldn't seem to make things go their way no matter how hard they tried, some who rose from adversity, some who just didn't try. Grover was one of the latter. I won't use his last name because family still lives around here, but he was to give us one of those stories that has brought grins and chuckles to a couple of generations.

He lived in Eden. Trees shaded that little settlement beside the lazy Yadkin. I suppose the river inspired him to be as lazy as lazy could be, but even when it wasn't lazy and went wild, Grover just watched it go by.

Houses, commercial and residential, were scattered along the railroad tracks and the hills above in a cluster that roughly centered at the Southern Railway depot/freight office in Crutchfield. Dirt paths went haphazardly from door-to-door, and only the railroad property was painted, for the most part. For those traveling from Crutchfield to Elkin or Wilkesboro, our Burch Station was the next siding up the line.

A steep hill rose behind the settlement. Trees covered the rise until, just below the crest, an impressive Victorian mansion lifted shiny tin roofs over tree tops; two-storied with gingerbread trim around attic windows, wide-porched, and painted! Like a castle of old, the house stood above the lesser dwellings. His sister lived there.

Grover's habitation was an old harness room adjacent to the stables. It was furnished with discarded things from his mother; an iron bedstead, a marble-topped table, odd chairs. An old black stove stood on a sandbox sitting near the room's center, its smoke pipe guided upward and supported by wires to the window whose upper panes were tin rather than glass. A heavily worn church pew, long since replaced by one built in a factory, sat nearby along one wall. It was just right for an assortment of odd dishes and pans.

The whole of the harness room resembled a bachelor's bolthole, which, of course, it was. But Grover only needed it when he needed it - only used in inclement weather. Otherwise, Grover needed to be out and about securing his next meal.

All of his happy hours were spent in an old flat boat kept tied up to a tree by the river. Its near derelict state wasn't inviting to anyone else, but Grover made it his second home; or, I suspect, it was really his first choice. From its river side he fished; inside he hid his sippin' whiskey; nearby was a bed tick he could curl up in whenever he wanted, and from a chair on the deck he could lean back to ponder the ways of the world and the lives of his neighbors in Eden.

Only hunger spurred Grover into circulation. Credit was no longer negotiable in stores, so he had come to rely on the women of the nearby houses who were usually good for a biscuit with a piece of side meat or a plate of greens flavored with streaked meat. But when a solid meal was desired, Grover had to walk up the hill to the back door of his sister's house. There he would be fed, but the meal always came with a lecture on his sorry condition.

When hunger coincided with Sister's absence, he was assured of pantry privileges, and so begins this tale. One sunny spring morning, when he saw her boarding the "Up Train," he scooted up the path toward an unguarded pantry.

A well stocked pantry it was, too! He chose a canned meat, cranked off the lid, raided the bread box, and with knife in hand, he settled in to feed.

Needed salt. Then a little pepper. Then, with the entire contents spread on thick bread slices, he was soon the better of his feast. It was only when he was clearing away the crumbs, hiding the evidence of his presence, and was cleaning the knife that the empty tin caught his attention.

He gasped! Suddenly his stomach tied in knots. Knees buckling from shock, he hurredly descended the hill, staggered along the railroad tracks to Preacher Draughn's house where he implored comfort and a conversation with the Lord, because Grover was sure he was going to die.

Right there on the front porch the Preacher knelt with him. No finer praying had ever been heard in Crutchfield as the two men beseeched the Lord that His will not be done quite yet. Presently, the two rose from weary knees and settled into rocking chairs waiting for the end, whatever it might be. They rocked and waited while the sun sat westerly.

At sundown, Grover went home to his harness room contemplating his sin. That tin of dog food hadn't been so bad after all.

Then came the flood. High waters didn't come often, but when the river rose, it swept everything along in its currents. Grover's boat was washed down stream.

The Yadkin River was normally quiet, smooth, and always muddy, but heavy rains occasionally caused such swelling that the bottomlands were awash hill-to-hill. A time or two, Burch Station was within washing away while the Yadkin brought unbelievables floating down. Houses, sheds, whole trees. And once came animal cages from Wilkesboro Bottoms. A little monkey danced and chattered upon one cage, holding out his arms as child would. The water swept him on down river.

People from the mountains lost more than their homes in the floods; all their possessions were swept away, too. We gained "Lost John" (Jessie Ray) for a tenant that way. After torrential rains one spring, he and his family had come downstream looking for a new beginning, and my father, John Martin, allowed the Ray family to move into an old tenant house on the farm down by the Yadkin. It sat above the bottoms, and the Rays were willing to sharecrop.

Displaced people lower their demands and expectations; a good roof instead of none, an old wood burning cook stove instead of none, sack mattresses stuffed with straw or leaves were far better than nothing. And they had a home. From all around, clothing, bed covers, food, pots and pans; things they would need were gathered up and given to the Ray family. They became part of our community, our folks.

The gift of a fiddle lifted "Lost John" to the status of Neighborhood Treasure for he was a fiddling marvel. His fame spread far and wide; radio opened new worlds to his family - with "Lost John" as centerpiece. With his boys they grew into a musical group that won first prize in every Fiddlers Convention they entered.

When folk music collectors came around with tape recorders, "Lost John" made PBS and will be preserved as an Appalachian folk artist extraordinaire. His music will long be a fixture among the sounds of our time. While only those who actually saw him would recognize "Lost John;" his music will likely survive, but who he was will, no doubt, become lost as our time is replaced by another.

Peering at the world from under squinting eyelids that were fixed, immovable and just barely opening wide enough to see, "Lost John" had to tilt his head back to see in front of him, but limited sight didn't hamper his fiddlin'. With his fiddle in the crook of his left arm, bow singing back and forth across it, "Lost John" gave us folk music with an image not intended to be folksy; he just did the best he could with what he had been given and became part of us and our time.

When Matt Sneed built a fertilizer house beside the railroad tracks, Burch was more than a Southern Railway station: its houses and stores presented a village appearance to the world. Sneed's warehouse was just the newest building. It was a long, narrow thing right up next to the tracks and near the Section Foreman's house. Freight cars rolled down the siding and up so close that they were unloaded directly into the warehouse.

Farmers brought their families in wagons or trucks to purchase supplies, meet arrivals or wave to departures as the left the station, use the Railway Express office or the Post Office next to Williamson's General Merchandise.

By then the warehouse that Howell Carter built from his sawmillings was a fixture of Burch Station. It's the only structure to survive and still stands right on the edge of Route 268. Florence Carter did fine sewing in the Carter family rooms of the building where they lived after her father closed the sawmill. Her mother, Lizzie, also lived with them, and it was her job to move their cow from grassy patch to grassy patch bordering the highway, along the railroad, or among obliging neighbor yards - she seemed to always be holding the end of its chain.

Mr. Carter had a car sitting up on blocks over in one corner. I never saw it move. Inside at the front of the building near the highway was a 1-room store, and in back were the living quarters. It was just the three old folks living there since the Carter's only son had gone away.

Mr. Carter seemed to grow smaller as he sat through his days in his little store. It was composed of one wall of shelves and a counter, and he waited behind it with a speller and chemistry texts in his lap waiting like a patient spider to trap someone in talk. Train crews didn't have time for such

51

things and would holler at the old man for whatever they were after and leave hastily. He just wanted to talk to someone, I suppose. It was just him and the women.

Most of the hillside between the new highway that Carter's warehouse sat on and the railroad was owned by Matt Sneed. He built a large house and even larger barn just around the curve and raised a big family. The oldest son, William, was always at his father's side, driving the buggy, then a car, tending to business, always busy.

Will was put on a longer tether when he took a wife: Miss Gertie. They lived in a different house, but he reported for duty immediately after breakfast. There was no question of being his own man because his wife took a job and was out of the house; Matt had things needing doing.

Miss Gertie did well, becoming a buyer for J.C. Penney Company, and worked for years in Elkin while Will stayed on the farm tending to business. She was a power in the Little Richmond Church, especially with a singing voice that carried above all others. And she was equally a power throughout the community, always willing to help whoever might ask, all her long life of doing things well.

Burch Station began its decline when more and more people took to the highways in automobiles. With Elkin's stores so much more inviting and so close by, a matter of a few curvy miles along the River Road, and with growing numbers of cars to take the whole family if need be, and it usually was, carloads went by Burch Station to spend their Saturdays walking Main Street. And as the need for fertilizer from Sneed's warehouse was displaced by Brendle's Feed and Seed in Elkin, Burch Station soon became a victim of changing times.

So, the affairs of business in the Sneed households

shifted more to farming. The rich land along the river bottoms produced fine crops of tobacco, corn, and wheat, and Will became a good farmer. Unfortunately, he didn't outlive his father who married for the third time when he was in his late 90s, to Florence, who, as an old, old lady, still lived in her father's now so very quiet and run down warehouse on the edge of Route 268 at Burch Station.

Farming is often thought of as "the good life:" fresh air, the out-of-doors, living in communion with the earth. Will could be thought of as the model farmer in our area, but one day his way of life turned on him. While cutting grain, the oscillating teeth of his tractor-driven mower jammed, and in an attempt to free its cutters, the ends of three of his fingers were clipped off like wheat stalks.

It was a shattering blow to such a hard working man, one who had been a long time fixture around Burch Station. But to be cut down in middle age with much of his life ahead was the greater tragedy. Laatr, Will lingered through an amputation after a foot developed gangrene and died while his father lived on with his third wife, Florence, to be an old, old man of over 100 years.

Everyone catered to Grandpa Sneed, the oldest among several old men in our community at the time, and he was finally laid to rest in the Sneed plot in the Little Richmond Cemetery after more than a century of living.

Miss Gertie outlived them all and finally was unable to continue her post in the church. She passed that mantle on to a new generation near the end of the 20th century as life went on, as it always does, all around us.

Along about the time that Burch Station was in its prime, a new generation was coming along who needed their ABCs, syllables, and arithmetic drilled into the community's new scholars; back then, spelling and hand-writing were considered essential.

When the big Spell Down one year brought all the best spellers together at the end of term, the Martin family had a prize winner. Young Dot won a five dollar gold piece, but her pleasure was of short duration; her parents, John and Alice, marched her into the Bank of Elkin to deposit the treasure.

That was me, and no prouder speller the world had ever seen, but no more disappointed a child had ever lived when the bank went bust. Closed its doors. And my gold piece.... Gone, too. And the Spelling Champion went on wearing made-overs.

While visiting the Carters for a fitting one day, the ladies left the Speller to passtime with the "old man." In his little store, always on the sly about who could do what, Mr. Carter had heard about my winnings.

"Well, Dot. I hear you can spell," prompted a modest assent. "Spell immediate."

"Im-me-di-ate."

"Right you are! Now spell caoutchouc."

"Coo-chook... Never heard of it."

With the old man's grin, I suddenly knew a little more about why the train crewmen hollered at him. They were always in a hurry, no time for his shenanigans. Mr. Carter was sharp, and he liked to prick anyone within range. Curiosity piqued, I discovered that the word really was in Webster's Dictionary, and I learned a new word for rubber.

But, like everyone else, I walked a little more wary of the old man after that. I didn't want to lose my champion speller's mantle so quickly or easily again.

Some years later after I went to college, I had the

occasion to be in Mr. Carter's store, and he put the needle to me again asking, "Dottie, now that you've been to college, can you tell me the formula for water?"

Howell Carter's warehouse and store at Burch Station c. 1938

That one I knew, but I thought about it and replied, "H - 2 - O."

"That's right," he grinned, "two parts hydagene and one part oxygene."

When I Was Little

Churning was a constant when I was a little girl. Before refrigerators, milk was cooled in basements, dry wells, spring houses, or water tubs. If you had one, the coldest place in the house was the icebox, and each day or so the ice man would come by. If you had enough money to buy ice, you could keep milk, butter and other perishables cool with a block or two. Our icebox was on the back porch, and in its cold water jars of milk waited to be separated into cream and to be churned into butter.

Up and down, up and down - farm women earned their keep with churn handle in hand. Then squeezing milk from the butter, then pressing the butter into molds fashioned it into cakes of about a pound in weight. With milking a twice-a-day thing, day after day and no end in sight, there was churning to do all the time.

Truly, Grandpa married labor-saving devices; wives were replaceable as he demonstrated with his three Elizabeths. With the third one, theirs was a big family, and big families ate a lot of three squares every day. Along with churning, cooking and cleaning up afterward, each day was dominated by the kitchen for country wives.

But when Grandma Dell came to visit, churning turned into wonderful entertainment. As she worked the dasher up and down, her stories charmed us.

We'd say, "Do the name song, Gramma." And she'd chant in time with each stroke of the dasher,

> "Katy, Katy Cath'rine, Augusta Jane,
> Sally, Sukey, Cindy Ann, Watson Crane.
> Mirandy Ann Eleanor, Eleanor Ann,
> Sugar Tea Lump and Honey Tea Can.
> Camellia John, Claricey Caroline,
> Louisey Vincent Gilchrist."

Her songs and stories that never came from books kept us entranced. She had a gift; the Hamlin gift of music and story-telling. After supper the Hamlins picked up fiddles, guitars, banjos, autoharps and "made music" together.

In summer, children clustered about the bean stringing elders; charmed by their songs and stories, never realizing that they were being *taught*. It was painless instruction and lots of fun.

In winter the group gathered around the hearth. Twenty verses of "Froggie Went A-Courting" suited the youngsters; "Barb'ry Ellen" suited young adults. Most were narratives with a pointed moral: loved or unloved, all end in the church yard.

Hymnals were a fixture and always near to hand. The shaped notes of the hymns were learned and followed closely; "singing schools" flourished. We entertained ourselves and shared our lives with all who joined in. It was our way of socializing and learning.

And, as you might expect, our feelings for the world we lived in were deep and strong. When little chicks were found dead, our hearts were filled with grief that such a young thing had already lost its life. We children gave the

Ben preached,
Wiley sang,
Lucille wept,
I was grave digger.

"diddles" fine funerals; preaching, singing, and somber grave digging followed by placing of flowers and crosses, too.

Do coming events cast their shadows before their arrival?

As the years unfolded, one of those children became a church organist/pianist and spent more than fifty years playing for funerals. The proceedings of each little chick laid to rest during my childhood guided me through life's sad moments, including my own parents who came to their ends much too soon for me. I played for each of them, my last farewell to Mama and Daddy.

Talk. A means of enriching the daily routine when people were never too busy to exchange words, share news, pass messages along; and every family had stories that were treasured. To hear one of my favorites, Gramma Dell would, when suitably begged, recount her memories of Eng and Chang, a story that kept all of us enthralled.

The Siamese Twins, joined at the side from birth, were often in the news and exhibited all over the world. They were famous, and their grave in White Plains, North Carolina, is not too far from the Hamlin Ford. While alive they would occasionally stop for a neighborly visit when driving the road by the Hamlin home.

"When I was just a little girl," Gramma Dell would begin, "I watched them accommodate their descent from the buggy seat. Now that was a sight. It was my job to place two chairs together for them to sit, and I did that just as quickly as I could so that I could watch their unique progress across the yard, up the steps, and their final coordinated sit into my chairs."

I could see them in her descriptions; what marvels they must have been. She told me that they were the world's original Siamese Twins. Eng and Chang, named for "right" and "left", were born on a houseboat in what was then Siam on May 11, 1811. Viewed as an evil omen, a curse on the land, they drew the king's wrath, and King Rama II ordered them killed, but to escape from that order and eventually to arrive in America was their destiny rather than an unknown grave.

They were fishermen and helped their father until he

Grandma Dell knew Eng and Chang

died when they were about eight years old. First fishermen, then peddlers, then they raised ducks for eggs to sell, a meager existence in any case. Then, when just 18, they left Siam behind. With a contract in hand, they were on a ship bound for America. They went on tour around the country and befriended an American family, whose name, Bunker, they took for their own. An admission fee of fifty cents per person, an astounding sum for 1829, was sufficient to make them both wealthy men. In just nine years they had forty thousand dollars each and decided to retire to the mountains of Wilkes County, North Carolina.

They were said to have been searching for the garden spot of the world and chose some three hundred acres flowing with several streams and springs in the Traphill area known as Long Bottom. They built a house with a wrap-around porch on the gentle slope of a meadow opposite the southern prominence of the Blue Ridge Mountains near Stone Mountain. There they met sisters of a neighboring farm, Sarah and Adelaide Yates.

On April 13, 1843, Sarah married Eng while Adelaide married Chang over many objections from family, friends and community. Eng fathered eleven children; Chang just ten.

As their families grew, their shared house was deemed too small, and the twins bought land in the White Plains community of Surry County where they lived out their days. Each sister had her own house, separated a short distance apart, and a regular schedule was kept; three days in Sarah's house, then three in Adelaide's. The seventh? I suppose that was each Sunday of the week, and their whole family got together somewhere.

The uniqueness of the Siamese Twins served them well. When times were tough and they needed money, they simply went on tour and filled their purses. Eng and Chang, two men attached just below the rib cage, were known to quarrel and to become embroiled in fierce brawls. They smoked and chewed tobacco, and went to sleep and awoke at the same time.

Chang's paralyzing stroke during 1870 became an extra burden his brother carried for four years. Then, on a cold January night, Chang became ill. The two of them lay down together as they had all their lives. In a few hours, Chang died. Eng followed him a few hours later.

Separated later, doctors discovered that they shared a common liver. Sadly, they were buried in separate coffins and were later moved to a cemetery in White Plains to join their wives.

Hands. Hands were never empty during my childhood. Men whittled or mended shoes or worked the lines, traces, and harnesses of their mules. Boys learned at their father's side. Women did marvels with needles and thread. Young girls were taught embroidery stitches, knitting, crochet, tatting and stitchery. When one got her own work basket, she began to fill a Hope Chest with the things she made.

Patches for quilt-making were exchanged - enough of a pattern to complete a design was a pressing matter! Any old colors, bits and pieces of cloth, went into a Crazy Quilt, but a Wedding Ring quilt was assembled from the finest cloth available and each patch counted. Then, many patches were joined to create the ring pattern, and when enough rings were made and stitched together, the top of a quilt was finished.

Then a lining to back the quilt and padding to go between the top and back were fastened into a frame that made the assembly ready for quilting. Each tiny, even stitch was pushed through all the layers - a job requiring a thimble, waxed thread, and plenty of push.

Quiltings were social occasions when neighbors assembled around the frame and helped get the job done. Patterns were compared, gift quilts made for newlyweds, commemorative quilts made to acknowledge a special event, even quilts to be raffled when money was raised for community needs.

When homes burned, and they all too often did, everybody in the community pitched in to help. Everyone knew that bad luck could come their way, too, and helping in time of need was a gift both given and received. A day's work among neighbors who raised a new house from the ashes, or raised a barn where one was needed, was worth much more than a day's work. Everyone knew that doing a good job took time, and they were accustomed to giving their best.

Preachers were paid with household needs. So were doctors. A day's work given was worth more than a cold fifty-cent piece when money was short. People were concerned with "basic needs," food, shelter, firewood, protection for their livestock, and since most needs simply could not be bought, the giving of one's time was far more appreciated than money. Wonderful works such as a quilt couldn't be bought, but they became gifts used for a lifetime and more.

"Neighbor" was a word that covered an interwoven social web - sharing was the basic ingredient that held communities together. Then came the Great Depression; it placed much of America, even our time-honored mode of country living, in a state of change.

Franklin D. Roosevelt said that fear itself was no longer to be feared. We Americans, as a nation, learned from his radio "fireside chats" that we could build a better

America. Radio carried his words to the far corners of this country, and government programs such as the Civilian Conservation Corps from the WPA was a new pattern of government assistance that many men participated in. And along came change.

As economic stagnation stirred into new life, money began to circulate. Jobs earned pay, and a man with money in his pocket walked proud. "Neighbor" lost much of its previous meaning, and a job well done got lost in the pursuit of more money.

The Depression was really rough on farmers. Sometimes it took gathering up chickens for sale at whatever you could get to make payments, and anyone who owed money stood the very real chance of having a repossessor show up with an eviction notice. It took pulling together, and when the farmer's co-operatives began around 1933, it was tough to hand over that $5 bill for a share of stock in it. But you had to. There wasn't much else a farmer could do; it took money and supplies to raise crops that didn't pay until fall-of-the-year, and buying what you needed at top dollar along the way meant that you couldn't make much after paying bills. So, you stayed in debt; paying off one just to make another. The co-ops meant having what you needed at lower prices and on credit.

Credit was hard to get elsewhere, and people didn't like doing business with banks; just one bad year was all it took to lose everything you'd worked all your life to build. So, with their business fallen off, banks had a hard time keeping money to loan, and even then, what you got had expensive interest rates attached. After the flood of crashes, nobody trusted banks anyway. Co-ops just made more sense and kept everything closer at hand.

Roosevelt made it all happen with the Farm Credit Act that established Production Credit Associations, P-C-A. The Farm Credit Act was tangled up in the "Triple A," the Agricultural Adjustment Agency that the Supreme Court ruled unconstitutional around that time. We had a "Triple A" office in Dobson, then a P-C-A with mostly the same people running it.

Those people who worked for the government had jobs, and most anyone with a job considered themselves fortunate. Money was hard to come by, and having regular pay of maybe four or five dollars a week was a luxury back then. But if you were a young hand laborer, you might could get ten cents an hour and dinner. That was good money, a dollar a day and a full stomach; not bad for a day's work.

Even though things didn't cost much, there sure wasn't much money going around, and if your children needed shoes or coats or textbooks requiring cash to be bought, a farmer could find himself broke and going to the P-C-A for another loan. You couldn't make any money, and you were always in debt.

When a farmer went to the P-C-A for a loan, he was evaluated to make sure he was good for it, and he had to put up twice the value of the loan as collateral. If a mule cost $100, he'd have to put up a couple of cows, too. So, there wasn't much defaulting because it was a big loss; you did whatever it took to survive, repay your loans and stay out of debt. But if a team of mules cost $400, and if that was what it took to farm, well, you just had to have'em.

The farmer's co-op had to make sure it didn't lose money, but it wasn't in the business of taking collateral; mostly, it was farmers helping other farmers who were worse off, helping figure out a way to get by that kept everyone going. You didn't hear much of the P-C-A taking farms; they mostly wanted farmers to stay in business. That was easier on everybody. But, sometimes, it was really tough for months on end, even years.

And there was always politics. What was the government going to do about this problem or that problem? But things moved ever so slowly, and what seemed like a good thing to campaign on might or might not be taken well by the voters if they thought it would cost too much.

Long about the mid-1930s, Clyde R. Hoey ran for a high office in North Carolina on a platform of free schoolbooks and old age pensions. By then, tuition and transportation were free for North Carolina children; the state provided buses, and taxes took care of school costs. But textbooks were expensive, and farming families traded books around for their children, and each one was looked after with biblical respect. After teaching for forty years, I've seen the respect for textbooks made them last for twe, three, four or more years reduce them to trash before a single school term is over. That would never have happened when education and books were important.

The second part of Hoey's campaign called for $30 per month for each old person, $15 from the state and $15 from the federal government, as a pension. Imagine that, $30 a month. Tells you how much money was worth back then, doesn't it?

Things sure have changed.

A river and railroad - a way in and a way out. There was a market for blackberries until Prohibition put North Carolina wineries out of business. That industry was gone by the time I was a little girl, but now it's slowly coming back, though of a very different character. Children back then could depend on summer earnings from hand picked blackberries, not to mention the wonderful pies and cobblers they made.

And there were red raspberries before the blackberries, muscadines afterward, peaches and cherries in late spring, pears in the summer, apples in the fall, blueberries occasionally, wild huckleberries whenever they could be found; fruit of all sorts that went into life as we knew it.

A few weeks after the berries we could augment our pickin' money with handing up tobacco during priming time. But for girls, that kind of work was mostly on the home farm and you didn't get paid. Girls didn't hire out, it just wasn't proper, but boys could make enough to buy new clothes and shoes of their choice rather than having to wear hand-me-downs when school started up. Girls learned to make dresses from feed sacks and to revise existing dresses to make them more fashionable and unrecognizable as hand-me-downs.

The railroad kept our lives flowing; fertilizer came in by the box car load in the spring, shipments of who knows what going who knows where left throughout the year. And some of that who knows what came to us.

When posters went up to invite the sinning public to be saved by Billy Sunday, a tidal wave of response swept through the area. A huge tobacco warehouse sandwiched between the river and railroad received a freight car load of folding chairs, another of sawdust, and a grand piano came next to companion the pulpit. It was revival time coming on the heels of summer Bible School.

Summertime brought tent revivals with local preachers who drew modest crowds looking for Godliness, but the big night at the warehouse came with anticipation; women fanned in the heat while men sweat. Us kids were just glad to be around anything exciting. A capacity crowd, packed in by ushers, awaited the Magic Moment while rousing gospel music flowed to the heavens. Then, God's representative came running down the sawdust trail and leaped upon the pulpit where he fought the (invisible) Devil. Winning that battle with the help of the Almighty, the Bible was thumped, and the word of God poured over everyone. Altar calls resembled a rush to catch a train. Lines formed, women wept, and miracles were performed.

In those days religion was taken seriously.

Hard Times

When the Depression came, horror tales were exchanged as the norm - everybody was affected: bank closings, brokers leaping from windows, unemployed people shuffling in soup lines. Hard Times! My father was told, "No job or go on three-quarter pay, deliver orders, drive a pick-up instead of a car," In effect, double work for less pay.

Nobody had any money, and what the automobile had started, the Great Depression finished at Burch Station. On "Relief Day" people *walked* to Dobson, the County

69

Seat, for free government food: dried beans, corn meal, flour. Cheese occasionally. Rice. When our school bus passed them in the morning, walkers were empty-handed; in the afternoon they carried precious bundles - sacks laid across men's shoulders, smaller bundles in hand, and however many miles they had to go to get home, it was their burden all the way.

Farmers had it a little easier. We could grow and can our food, and if a mule and wagon were on the place, we could ride while others had to walk. The whole country had stepped back about thirty years; where wagons had once been common and the accepted way of life, progress had passed them by when automobiles became transportation from which people waved on their way to who knows where. Now, like Mr. Carter's car sitting on blocks in his warehouse, cars weren't moving because there was no money to buy gasoline, even if there had been gasoline to buy. And when a precious tire had been patched for the last time, it made no difference that the other three could not hold air, ol' Tin Lizzy wasn't going anywhere.

Newspapers carried pictures of long lines at city soup kitchens. Able bodied men stood on corners trying to sell pencils, or apples, or whatever they could get their hands on. Hooverville shanty towns became common, and wry humor permeated song and story.

> Hoover's in the White House,
> Eating ham and eggs.
> While I'm eating fatback,
> That I had to beg.
>> It's hard times,
>> It's hard times.

70

Come here, little children,
And hush your crying.
Mama's making gravy,
I smell the meat a-fryin'.
It's hard times,
It's hard times.

You couldn't quit. Day after day brought its
troubles, and people found ways of making do. In our part
of the country, we were accustomed to hand-me-downs and
make-overs, and if anything was at all usable, it was. If not,
it became quilt makings, because nothing was wasted.

Children wore clothing made from flour bags and
feed sacks; underclothes were made from sugar bags.
Sheets were four sacks sewed together. Seamstresses did
many small miracles in cutting down and making over; one
lady made men's suits of Chatham woolen at five dollars a
suit - you furnished the cloth and buttons.

Some folks in town who had jobs did all right. The
Chatham Blankets mill in Elkin and the furniture factories
cut back, some closed, but for the most part, they were able
to stay open at some level. Nobody even thought about
raises, they were just glad to have a job, and lots of extra
hours were spent for no pay at all. If the mill closed, the
heart of Elkin would have stopped with it, and everyone
would have been much worse off. People tended to pull
together, but tempers grew tender as time went on. Times
were tough, and change was slow in coming.

Slowly the Roosevelt programs began to take hold.
Farmers were coaxed into smaller acreages of money crops,
(tobacco, cotton) and the idea of planned food growth took
hold. Price supports and government programs to improve

land use slowly influenced farmers who had previously grown whatever and how much they could, only to have to compete in flooded markets that drove prices down. Grumble as they would, that old law of supply and

Plowing was long days just to do it all again spring and summer.

demand didn't work in favor of hard work resulting in over-production. Less work managed better got the same amount of money. It didn't seem to make sense and took a while to sink in.

Nobody liked to admit it, but war put people back to work, and while men were away our women learned to work... for money this time. This changed our culture; Moms were a new breed and daughters learned early that women need not be silent behind the men. Earners were also spenders, as merchandisers quickly recognized, and the business world that was composed mostly of men increasingly turned their attention toward women. Billboards, radio and the new televisions had a new attitude; Papa was not the only one in the family to have a "say" any more.

The Big Woods

round on the other side, west of the courthouse in
Dobson, was the old Martin Hotel. That was my
Daddy's grandfather's place. Richard Martin, newly
married himself, had come to Dobson with his new bride
many years before and built the hotel. It was closed when
John, my father, showed the hotel to his new bride, Alice,
and by way of introducing her to his family, he told her that
his father, John Winston Churchill Martin, had once been
the Register of Deeds for the County, and that he and his
family had lived in the hotel during that time. But his
father's health failed, and they moved to a location on
Hamlin land on the Fisher River where he died before the
son who carried his name another generation was born.
Consequently, my Daddy never knew his Daddy, who was
buried on a bluff overlooking the river.

Richard Martin had five wives. Samuel was his first born, with Elizabeth Ayers. With his second wife, Elizabeth Morgan, a daughter and a son, Elizabeth and Colohil, were born. Richard's third marriage, to Elizabeth Kellam Smith, already with seven children, resulted in four more, Elizabeth, William, John Winston Churchill and Spencer. John was my grandfather, although J never saw him. The fourth son from his union with Aradella Hamlin was also named John Winston, my father, who was born after his father's passing. Richard later wed Mary Hampton, then Rosie Hampton Roby, neither producing children. This writing in Richard's hand, still a young man then, is a family treasure.

Rockingham County, Moratur
March 27th 1835
Samuel Pleasant Thumler Martin

This breastpin is given to you for a memorial of an afflicted Father and a departed Mother.

When this you see them from me mind,
Your afflictedes Father you've left behind,
And that your Mothers truly on the grave with rest.
But its hoped her spirit is in eternal bliss.
Then let us serve the Lord while here below,
So that we may meet with her, to part no more.

By your affectionate Father
Rich Martin

Irene, Tom and Bessie's daughter, told of seeing Richard on his walks around Dobson, with his gold headed walking cane in hand. He did greeting and entertaining and taking of money at the hotel while the women did the work. When Richard got old, the running of the hotel was left to his son, John Winston Churchill Martin, and his wife, Aradella Hamlin, my grandparents. I'm told that John was a smart man, but he loved to drink, and he got into such a shape that he couldn't do either job, run the hotel or be Register of Deeds. He got the shakes, and they had to close the hotel. He lost his job with the county, too.

A deed still exists that shows that John Winston Martin sold the Martin hotel to a man named Dobson. Some years later that structure was torn down.

After they moved into a tiny house down on Fisher River, John Winston was sent off to be dried out. He had four living children, and his wife was expecting another, my Daddy, who maintained that, no, it wasn't the drink that killed his father because he had gotten better. What happened was that he got the "bloody flux," another summer disease that killed by dehydration and dysentery.

John Winston's and Dell Hamlin Martin's oldest child, Newton, stood by his Daddy's grave and said, "Don't cry Mammy, I'll be your man." And he was. He and Tom, a year or two younger, went to work and worked like Trojans. They raised tobacco and worked for farmers around, never asking for help; they went right out in the fields and tuckered in.

Daddy said that when he was twelve years old, he was tending eight tobacco barns in a row, wood burning barns that he had to cut wood for and watch all night long every night they were curing. They had the wood dragged up to the barns, and he'd lay his ax to it, stoke up the fires of one barn, put his ax on his shoulder, walk to the next barn and cut wood for it right on. By the time he was finished with the eighth barn, it was time to tend the fire of the first one.

He was a marvelous hand with an ax; he cut his line just as true as could be. Long practice and starting early in life did it. Good training. Daddy could use either hand for most things. Chips would fly from his ax, right cut, left cut, but he picked a banjo only with his left hand and wrote with his right hand.

Later on he got some high school. His brothers sent him to board in Dobson. Sometime along in there, Newt and Tom bought land in Salem Fork; it was called the "Big Woods" then. The place had a small house on the property, and they decided to put a store in it. That little house became their home. After schooling, young John Winston boarded with people around nearby and ran that store right by himself, kept the books and everything, until his older brothers came along and joined him after the farming season ended. At first, the store was just stocked shelves in one room of the house, but they soon built a square, box shaped store nearby right on the edge of the road. That building had a basement under it that they used for storing tobacco.

The Martin brothers became successful merchants. They built another store, much bigger than that first store, then built a mansion across the Dobson road from it. They moved into the fine new house in 1924. Newton didn't marry until late in life and had no children. By the time that he and Miss Kizzie Bray finally tied the knot, Tom and Bessie had several children, and Newton thought as much of them as if they were his own. Joyce came along just after the Martins moved into their fine home, and then Ray. He was the last child in Tom and Bessie's family.

Their first child, Spencer, had died as an infant. After him came Irene, then Hazel, Lora, Joyce, then Ray.

Spencer is buried in the Baptist church grave-yard up the road from the Martin Brothers' store toward Twin Oaks, what we referred to as Kizzie's church. At that time the Salem Fork Christian Church that the Martin brothers helped found had no graves in its cemetery, and Bessie didn't want Spencer to be lonely. Since then, the Martins have mostly been laid to rest in the Salem Fork cemetery, and Spencer lies elsewhere far from family.

Martin children of two families, all grown up c. 1940. Lora and Lucille (front l to r), then Irene and Joyce, Ben and Ray in our front yard in Little Richmond.

Newton and Kizzie courted for the longest time. She was an old maid school teacher, and he was often heard to say that they had set a date. Well, every time that marriage got into the air, Bessie would turn to in a flurry of activity getting ready for the wedding, washing and ironing and cleaning, and it wouldn't happen. Time and again that happened, until finally the day came. Newton and Kizzie were finally wed, and with a new, rather determined wife in the Martin mansion, Tom and Bessie soon packed up and moved out. There was that twelve room mansion designed for a big family, one that had always had the laughter and play of children, now mostly empty with just an older couple sitting by the fire looking at each other.

Tom measured out a place and built a new house for his family across the road and few hundred yards toward Dobson from the store. The small house that had served as their first store had been torn down by then, and between its location and the box store was where Tom chose to set the foundation. He had benefit of the well that had provided water during their previous residence. He built a fine wood frame house, two stories, with a broad porch that viewed the Dobson road from the south side all the way from the mansion on the knoll to the left into the woods far to the right toward Dobson. Mostly woods and some open fields lay on both sides of the road at the time.

Tom and Bessie now occupied the third house the Martin brothers were associated with upon relocating to the Big Woods. Their brother Richard had located further on toward Mountain Park and raised his family on a farm carved out of the same Big Woods, but on the western edge, while Newton and Tom remained on the eastern edge in what became known as Salem Fork. Richard and his family had a store, too, but much smaller than the spacious Martin Brothers store, which was the last mercantile structure put up by Newt and Tom. Two of Richard's daughters, Pauline and Gladys, stayed around and helped with Richard's store and raised their families there as well.

Richard's family was filled with children, too. I can't name them all, but there was a girl named Bessie, then Carl,

Bill, another boy I think, and Gladys and Pauline as the youngest. The various Martin families and their stores helped lay the foundation of the Salem Fork community as it came to be. And there were children galore. We were a prolific family of hard workers who were always able to keep things together.

This was where John Martin brought Miss Alice, his new bride. Well, Mama came from a family of means in East Bend who had a fine twelve room town house with a telephone in it. She was used to living good and had some worth of her own from her previous marriage to Mr. Cox. The Big Woods wasn't her cup of tea. So, she went home to visit and pouted a bit while Daddy came down into the Little Richmond community looking around. Previously, he had boarded at the Burch Hotel when he sold fertilizer at Burch Station, so he knew the area. One of the Burch men had built a fine, solid house down the road from the Burch Hotel at the turn of the century. It was just a few years old at the time Daddy came looking at it. The young couple it was built for had decided that they didn't want to live there and had moved on.

So, Daddy bought it, and Miss Alice came along, and they lived all their married life the house that became my home. The house suited her because it had a telephone and wasn't far from Burch Station. She could turn the crank and central would connect her to someone who had a phone. Not many people had telephones, so this was an added attraction for Miss Alice.

And just a little way down the road she could get on the train and go to Elkin or Wilkesboro or East Bend or Winston-Salem. Little Richmond wasn't nearly as confining as Salem Fork.

Lucille, Mama and me, 1921

For the first four years, she was without children.
They had decided that they weren't going to have any
children, so they were about to adopt a little boy and had
gone so far as to bring him here to get acquainted. Then she
turned up pregnant. They let the people have their little boy
back, and Mama and Daddy had me, November 19, 1918.

I came along just in time to keep Daddy from being
a soldier in the first world war. Will Sneed, down the road
toward Burch Station, had been in the first draft that came
through this part of the country, and if John Martin had no
children, he would have been in the next draft. But, the war
ended about then.

I was born in this house, and up through my tenth birthday, I went to school in the two-room Little Richmond School House a mile or so up the road toward Twin Oaks. The new brick school house replaced it in 1927. What a fine new school house that was.

All around here, there wasn't much open farm land. It was mostly wooded with a string of uncommonly stately homes along the ridge. From the Burch public house and stables down to the Rusk Post Office and Mr. Wilmoth's house just beyond, then Grandpa Chappell's house, and the Sneed house and on down the hill to Burch Station, this area was quite a prominent little neighborhood. Wherever she might have liked to have lived, Miss Alice made Little Richmond her home. John would likely have rather lived nearer his brothers in the Big Woods, but his branch of the Martin family was established in Little Richmond.

And of course, it became my home as well, along with Lucille and Ben.

Lucille, Ben and me at home, Little Richmond c. 1927

Family Connections

My grandfather, W. A. Martin, a merchant in East Bend, had an older daughter than my mother, Alice. Her name was Bessie. She was wed to Robert Cox. The Cox family was prominent and lived in the vicinity of Rural Hall. They owned very beautiful property; they dealt in timber, had stock in a toll bridge across the Yadkin River and had other money earning enterprises.

It was an advantageous marriage, but Bessie did not live long. She died of appendicitis, sometimes called colic. Not much was known about internal medicine in those days, so when she got sick, she died rather quickly. That was before the year 1900.

Mr. Cox came back to East Bend and looked at the younger sister, Alice, but she wasn't quite old enough for marriage, and she needed a little finishing. So, her father

sent her to the Salem
Academy in Old Salem, now
Winston-Salem, for a couple
of terms. Salem Academy is
still there, a prestigious
school.

After she finished,
Alice became a very young
bride to Mr. Cox, the second
Martin girl to become Mrs.
Robert Cox. She went to
live on the plantation with
its gracious white brick home
of two stories and columns,
a separate cook-house
connected to the main house
with a covered walkway, and

*W. A. and Flora Martin
East Bend, North Carolina
c.1935*

an expanse of land spread around it. The location was on
beyond East Bend. On the property was the house where
Alice and Mr. Cox lived. It is now the club house of a
country club. There was also a family graveyard with a rock
wall around it. It's still there.

Mr. Cox operated the family sawmill. Alice had help
in the house; her job was overseeing the preparation of food
for all the hands who worked in the sawmill. So, the two of
them were kept busy with their work.

It was along during this time that Grandpa Cox had
Alice pick out a big walnut tree on the property. They cut it
down and sawed it into lumber, finished it up nicely, and had
a local cabinet maker build the dining table and buffet that I
later grew up with in the Martin house. Those pieces of
solid walnut are now in my son, Alex's, house.

83

Mr. Cox and Alice had a child named Romulus, and pictures show him to have been a pretty baby. It was during the second summer that children were weaned, and during that summer he ate something that didn't agree with him. Perhaps it was roasted corn at a tobacco barn, but whatever it was, the child went into severe dysentery; he became

dehydrated and died. A lot of children died in this manner back then. This was the time before refrigerators and the medications that now can easily take care of such things.

Not too much longer after that, Mr. Cox was standing in the kitchen door one morning before breakfast, talking to Alice who was putting the meal on the table. Without a hint of warning, he dropped dead in his tracks.

Now, here was Alice, a very young widow having lost her child, too. So, she came back home to East Bend and went to work in her father's store. That was where John Winston Martin, my father, came along selling shoes. He always said it was the sunbonnet that first caught his attention. In time he learned that she was the young Mrs. Cox, a very pretty woman. She had been left well off, and it wasn't long before they were courting and decided to get married. It was 1911 or so.

My Daddy got Clain Barker's Daddy to ride with him from Crutchfield to East Bend so that he could bring the horse and buggy back while the marriage went on what little honeymooning they did, and so forth. The newlyweds rode the train back up to Crutchfield where Daddy got his horse and buggy back from Mr. Barker, then drove on to Salem Fork with his new wife. Crutchfield was close to where Mr. Barker lived, and it was also closer to Dobson than making the trip from Burch Station.

Dobson was the county seat, and John's roots connected with other prominent families, Hamlin and Freeman in particular, who lived in the town. They did quite a bit of visiting around, meeting family here and there, especially in Dobson.

Daddy and Mama, 1932

I can remember Mama saying that they went to visit old Judge Freeman who was sitting in front of his marble fireplace and hearth. He put a chew of tobacco in his mouth and presently produced a big pitoo that splattered all over that fine hearth. The ladies of the house oooed and ahhhed, then came and washed the hearth; they didn't want tobacco stained marble. Of course the Judge was supposed to spit into the fire, but.... The son, Robert Freeman, was a lawyer in Dobson, and the newlyweds visited with him, too.

Hamlin History: The 1830 census of our area lists families with the Hamblen (different spelling) family name and includes Stephen and William in Surry County, North Carolina, and Thomas in Rockingham County. Stephen is listed in the 30-40 age group, William in the 40-50, and Thomas is listed as 50-60. This indicates that they could have been brothers, or that Thomas may have been the father of the other two. Thomas was a blacksmith noted for gun making, so he must have had some steel working knowledge employed with his forge.

Other records list Thomas Vestal Hamlin (1820-1885) as born in Rockingham County. He is presumed to be the son of the elder Thomas. He married Sarah Jane Askew (1824-1907) on the 13th day of November, 1844. Eight children from this union produced four boys and four girls. The fourth child, Aradella, was the second girl following two boys. Aradella was my Grandmother.

The two oldest boys, Richard "Dick" Hamlin and Pete, went to Texas during the time that the Lone Star State offered a wild west kind of invitation. There were skirmishes with Indians and tall tales about Pecos Bill and other Texas legends. Settlers had a lot of wide open spaces, the sort of things that would attract my father for a visit when he was a young man.

It could be that one Stephen Martin was drawn to Texas during the time of the Alamo. That name is listed among the participants, and who knows, he might be a relative.

The eighth child of Thomas and Sarah, Stephen Crawley Hamlin, became a fiddle player who continued the traditions of the southern mountain music we knew in our part of western North Carolina.

The Hamblen name became transliterated over time, becoming Hamlin as I learned it, and according to the encyclopedia, Surry County, where most of the Hamlins in Gramma Dell's line settled, was divided in 1789; its previous parts were renamed as new counties. The Yadkin River was a natural dividing line that produced Yadkin County from the south bank and to the west. Stokes County was made adjoining Surry to the east as another county along Virginia's southern boundary.

Crawley Hamlin, fiddler c. 1932

The first county seat was Rockford on the Fisher River, literally a rocky ford across bank-to-bank shallows. A brick courthouse was the seat of Surry County business

87

until 1853 when the county seat was moved to Dobson. The first courthouse in this new location was built in 1853, later remodeled and enlarged in 1916.

During the three years the Dobson courthouse was a-building, court was held in the Martin Hotel across the street. The new courthouse was a fine stone structure that anyone can inspect to this day. It became the crossroads of the county and felt the steps of ever-so-many of our folks. Dusty, old papers still in its confines tell of their lives.

The Martin Hotel sat facing the west entrance of the courthouse on the corner of Crutchfield Street. Beside it was the Llewellyn house, a fine home. Across the street southwardly stood the Kenlin Hotel, and diagonally across the intersection of Crutchfield and Atkins Street stood the Norman Hotel. The Norman Hotel was a fine stone building with a tall hedge between it and the street. The Kenlin Hotel was the last of the Dobson hotels. It served the courthouse personnel for decades.

My second daughter, Charlene, knew this hotel and was among the last of its patrons. She graduated from Dobson's high school in 1960, and because she was experiencing stomach ailments, Charlene took her lunch there. The school cafeteria food was probably about 35-cents, but of institutional character and usually quite greasy. For $1.25 each day, Charlene received a well prepared meal with a slice of pie and did so among the business people of Dobson, especially those who worked at the courthouse. It seemed to be the right thing to do. Her stomach problems subsided.

In my memory, Big Jim was the colored caretaker of the Llewellyn place. He and the hotel were fixtures of hotel life in Dobson for many, many years. But time went by, and both the Martin and Llewellyn Hotels became derelict and were torn down. So did the Norman in time, followed by Charlene's lunchery. And Big Jim left Dobson's hotel era as well.

His little house that sat behind the Llewellyn was put up for free to anyone who would move it. Otherwise, its fate was the same. And do you know, they brought in devices to lift that house and towed it with a tractor down Crutchfield Street a few blocks to its new residence. To this day, Big Jim's house has sat behind the Norman house just a block off Highway 601 through Dobson. It's amazing what survives and what doesn't.

Donnaha

When I was a child, we rode the "Down Train" as far as Donnaha when Mama and I went to East Bend. We would go down to Burch and get on the afternoon train, then go through all the little stops until we got to Donnaha. That's where the railroad leaves the Yadkin River. On the way back, we took the "Up Train" in the morning back to Burch.

The tracks ran along the north bank of the river all the way from Wilkesboro to Winston-Salem and Greensboro. At the big bend where the Yadkin turns south is Donnaha. Once upon a time it was Donnaha Station, much like Burch Station and Crutchfield. There was also a little Southern Railroad station at Siloam. All of the station buildings along the railroad seemed to have been cut from the same cloth, so to speak. Later on, when the railroad stopped its passenger and freight service to that station, a farmer bought the Siloam Station and moved it onto his property.

An Indian town once stood on the broad river bottoms at Donnaha. As I remember the stories about it, the Saura Indians were the inhabitants, and they gave their name to the Saura Town Mountain, a ridge of hills nearby. The Yadkin bends sharply south, and as I understand it, Saura Town was on the north side in the broad bottoms. The Indians farmed the bottoms, no doubt, as they were quite civil. I don't know what happened to them, but I suspect that they were assimilated into the settlers because they weren't part of the Cherokee. It could be that they were a branch of the Lumbee Indians who inhabited what became the surrounds of Lumberton on down toward the coast.

The Yadkin River makes the division between Yadkin and Forsyth Counties, and then Davidson and Davie Counties, as it heads into High Rock Lake. From the other side, out comes the Pee Dee River that runs all the way to the Atlantic Ocean through South Carolina.

When we got close to Donnaha, the conductor would always sing out, sometimes we'd sing along, too;

> "All off for Mt. Airy-y-y,
> Pilot Mountain,
> Walnut Co-o-ove.
> Don't forget your little packages."

Passengers for those destinations had to change at Donnaha Station. Those for Winston-Salem and Greensboro would stay on the train.

Donnaha bridge over the Yadkin River c. 1900,
washed away in the 1916 flood

When we got off the train at Donnaha, we rode with the mailman over to East Bend. It wasn't far, eight or ten miles, maybe less. The mail buggy was always at Donnaha to get East Bend's mail from the train. The mailman always had room for us, and he talked a blue streak.

"So, you're going to Grandpa's! A fine store he's got. I remember when your Mama waited on customers... before she married that mountain man...."

He and Mama talked about changes, everything was changing.

"Stamps are going up again, from two cents for a letter to three - and it won't be long before there won't be penny post cards any more. Goin' up a penny at a time so's people won't be able to afford the mail."

I wasn't interested in what was changing, I wanted to see East Bend. There were lots of things to see.

Grandpa's store was just the beginning for a country starved girl. I couldn't wait to get to town, but the mailman always seemed to be in no hurry. At first he drove a buggy, but when automobiles became the "in" thing, it was a mail truck we rode in and that didn't seem to be a bit faster.

Once we crossed the Yadkin on a steel bridge that looked much like the trestle across the Mitchell at Burch Station, I knew it wasn't far. That was along the main road from Winston to Rural Hall to East Bend, Route 67 now.

Before the railroad came along, East Bend was nearly as large as Winston. Then the Cape Fear and Yadkin Valley Railroad decided NOT to cross the Yadkin and bring the line into East Bend; well, that left the town high and dry, and the world went around it.

The railroad was built with convict labor and had consolidated with the Mt. Airy Railroad in 1879. That made a route from Richmond and Danville to North Wilkesboro. The name changed to "Southern" in 1894 on a 99 year lease.

Today, the short line starting at Rural Hall and ending at Roaring River is the Yadkin Valley Rail Road, just a one hundred mile remnant of the former Southern line. It operates without a schedule, up in the AM, down in the PM, more or less. No big, colorful steam engines anymore; just dingy little diesels pulling wood products, chicken feed, whatever its twenty-two customers need.

Changes: I've seen a lot of changes by now. Old timers I knew as a child are in the cemeteries and their children, now parents, are rapidly becoming old timers themselves. At eighty, I qualify as one: an old-timer, not something I wanted, it just happened. Time took care of it. I've taught many of the solid citizens of this area their A-B-Cs, geography, American history... a little music and art thrown in along the way. And I've played the final, solemn services for many old-timers, more than I care to think about; now its mostly my friends, and there aren't many of them left. What's really sad is to play the service for one of our citizens who I remember as a child.

One thing I've learned is that when people meet, how things are changing is always a main topic. While they talk, memories are sharpened about how things used to be. I suppose we sharpen our senses of human experiences common to our species, but time sure wreaks havoc on all things human.

Mama would step up into the mail truck for East Bend and not think a thing about it. It gave her transportation, freedom, to get where she wanted to go. Soon, mothers were appalled by the freedom of youth, how much freedom their children enjoyed. Young people got on trains or into cars and paid no mind to their elders. Change; we had been running slowly along when all of a sudden the whole world shifted into high gear and roared out of hearing distance.

The automobile brought about a new mind set...
everyone wanted to RIDE - go just to go. No more walking, no more hard labor; cars opened the way to new worlds
off somewhere from where young people were. Cars powered dreams: power to
move at will came to
stay, and "His" and
"Hers" no longer
meant towels! Where
income had once been
"His," two pay checks
came to dictate bigger
houses with double
garage space so that

Jacked up '40 Ford, haulin' space,
a little nearer Heaven on Sunday

"His" and "Hers" had their own mobility. That was a
profound change. Values were altered forever. Cars took
people off to who knows where, and "His" and "Hers" time
spent together without supervision changed the role of
parents and home. Mobility put parents and home into life's
back seat with youth driving. That was change as big as it
could get.

Of course it all had to be paid for. So, along came
convenience and less structured time use that added up to
easy credit that eroded patterns of thrift.... Yep, the times
changed, that's for sure; careening along in high gear for a
while, then up went the car on dusty blocks because there
was no gas or money. Then along came another war that
permanently removed the blocks, and we've been careening
along in high gear ever since.

The Huff Buggy works in East Bend is a good
example. It opened its doors in 1873 and made fine rigs that
were turned out until 1920. What had been a home town

industry that put food on the tables of several families folded as everyone rushed to buy cars. Cars, rare up until then, became the norm. Buggies couldn't compete with Henry Ford's mass produced Model T that was cheaper and could also be fixed with pliers and wire. And it could go most anytime without the inconvenience of hitching up the horse-power. When it stopped you just left it where it was; no unhitching and feeding the horsepower.

The railroad by-passing East Bend and drivers of cars seeing beyond this little town so changed it that East Bend became little more than a local farmer's supply town. Since it was my mother's home town and we visited often, I got to know it and its people pretty well, especially my family whom we visited with some regularity.

I've already mentioned the Cox connection, that was before my Daddy met Miss Alice, and of course, long before me. It's for sure that if Mr. Cox had lived, I wouldn't be telling all this, because there would not have been a me. And if my half-brother Romulus had lived, I suspect that there would be a lot more to tell about the Coxes, a lot more than a little grave surrounded by a rock wall down near Rural Hall.

We visited Mama's sisters, Aunt Elsie and Aunt Polly, and lots more Martins. Mr. W. A. Martin, Mama's Daddy, was a prominent man in the community. He had a fine house and a good sized store across the street that provided farmers, and most everyone else in East Bend, with what they were looking for.

Mr. W. A. was a hard working man with a hard working family of fine folks. He was active in their church, too, a particularly devout man as it turned out. Grandma Flora spent her whole life right by him, mothered all the children, took care of what needed taking care of, and when Mr. W. A. was laid to rest, the reading of his last will and testament left everything to the church. Grandma Flora no longer had her house, the store, or anything.

My family in East Bend, 1944. That's me holding Charlene. Daddy and Mama on my right. W. A. and Flora Martin, my grandparents, on my left. In front (l to r) are Michaela, Johnny on a tricycle and Ruth Ann York, another of the Martin grandchildren.

I suppose that Mr. W. A. reckoned that the Lord would provide for her and the children, and that His calling for worldly goods was more important than a husband looking out for a wife and family after he was gone. Grandma Flora spent several years, and all of her last days, living here with one daughter for a while, living there with another daughter for a while, and left this world without sleeping a single night in her own bed after the settling up was done. Funny how things turn out sometimes.

Oh! The stories that the Martins could tell. As a child I was enthralled with their stories about our French heritage, about Chief Donnahoo and Betty Pledge, the Poindexters and romance. There were patriots of the Revolution in my ancestry, men, women and little girls, too. There were sea captains. There were broken hearts and fallen Civil War sweethearts, and I was to see some fascinating stories played out in my lifetime as well. Since then, a lot of the historical details have been compiled that fleshes out the people and their lives, mostly by Kay Alley of East Bend.

Poindexter is the American version of Poingdestre, French. Once there was a Peter Poingdestre who lived in the Parish of St. Saviours on the Isle of Jersey. That was during the early 1300s. Apparently, the island changed hands, French then English, and back and forth some more during the subsequent centuries. His grandson, John, was a judge in the Royal Court on the island, and his son, also a John, became the Bailly of Jersey in 1424, an appointment by the King of England. He was the highest civil officer on the island. By then he lived on land purchased in the Parish of St. John, land that became known as the "Feif-es-Poingdestre."

John lived a long time, and his son George carried on the fiefdom as Lord of Poingdestre Manor. His son, another John, rose to become the Mayor of St. Saviours

Parish. His son, Edward, continued the line, and his son, Thomas was born in 1581. Thomas married Elizabeth Efford and fathered five children.

The third of their children, George, is in my direct line. He was a merchant ship owner and planter who emigrated to the Middle Plantation, Williamsburg, Virginia in 1657 and became America's first Poindexter. He was born on December the 23rd of 1627 on Swan Farm, St. Saviours Parish and died in New Kent County, Virginia in 1692. He might have gotten caught up in the in-fighting with the Royal Governor over tobacco prices that led to the Indian massacres of Bacon's Rebellion of the 1670s, but afterward, during 1685, he built the famous house known as Christ's Cross in New Kent County. It is one of the oldest houses, and the first brick house, in the area and has since been restored.

There's a story that George's father, Thomas, protested the oppression of the Catholic Church in his native land and became a Protestant. His family might have been among those exiled by the French King Charles who then established themselves as Englishmen on the Isle of Jersey just off the coast of France in the English Channel. George, so the story goes, fell in love with an English girl named Susannah. It was one of those nobility and peasant girl kinds of stories, and George's father forbade the marriage. To effect their separation, the elder Poingdestre presented his son with a handsome estate in the Royal Colony of Virginia and sent him off across the Atlantic to tend it.

That Land Grant was dated March the 15th, 1657 and accounted for three hundred-fifty acres in Gloucester County. Since George was the third son, English law provided that his eldest brother continued the line of Lord of Poingdestre Manor, and all the other children, including himself, got nothing. So, shipping off to America was the "in" thing to do if you were a young man seeking to make your mark on the world, or if Daddy was determined to forestall an unwanted marriage.

Well, Susannah set her heart on following George, and some time later she indentured herself as a servant for four years in exchange for passage to America. Young George learned of a ship to arrive with servants, and whether or not he knew of her intentions I don't know, perhaps it was all pre-arranged to avoid arousing suspicions of the young man's father, but I imagine that they rushed to each other's embrace. George paid the stipulated price for her indenture, and soon the two were wed. Thus began the first and only Poindexter line in America, so far as is known.

This rendition flows with romance and makes an entertaining story, but it appears that records exist showing that George and Susannah had three children in England. So, there couldn't have been a stern father trying to prevent a marriage. It had already happened. So, you have to be careful when trying to separate fact from fiction, and it might not be possible this far down stream. Anyway, their fourth child, another Thomas, was born in New Kent County, Virginia and lived just forty-four years. He married Sarah Crawford, and they had six children. Another Thomas, their fifth child, was born in 1705 in New Kent County. He relocated to Louisa County a little further west of New Kent sometime during his life and married Sarah Bond Veale. Well, along came another Thomas, their third of six children, and this Thomas Poindexter rose to become prominent in the Revolution. He was born in 1733 and lived a long and fruitful life of some seventy-four years and lies buried alongside his wife in Surry County, North Carolina, on a knoll overlooking the Yadkin River.

Thomas Jr. was well-heeled and married during his twenty-second year. Unfortunately, his Miss Sarah Hughes and her young child died within a year. Thomas went without a wife for the next five years, then sought the hand of Elizabeth (Betty) Pledge. Her parents provided the Indian connection in my ancestry.

Betty Pledge was the granddaughter of Donnahoo, Indian Chief. He had married Mary Wentworth, daughter of an English nobleman, a Mr. William Wentworth. One of their daughters married William Pledge, also a Virginian, and they had two children, Francis and Elizabeth. Elizabeth was known as Betty, and she has been recognized by the Daughters of the American Revolution, along with her husband, for their parts in forming our country.

At the time, it was 1760, the Cherokee were a powerful tribe from Iroquois extraction whose lands extended throughout the Appalachians from Virginia to Georgia. As the westward movement pushed them further into and beyond the mountains, along the way many friendly Indian tribes who were not Cherokee were assimilated into colonial families. That could account for the demise of the Saura Indians who were, perhaps Donnahoo's people.

Betty and her husband, Thomas Jr., had a large family of twelve children split evenly between boys and girls. Some were born in Virginia. An opportunity must have presented itself in North Carolina, and the remainder of their children were born in this state. Thomas Jr. purchased four hundred forty-three acres of land for the sum of three hundred-twenty British Pounds. The land was known as "Bailie Bottoms" and lay in the bend of the Yadkin River across from what became the Donnaha Railroad Station. He moved his family from Goochland County, Virginia, just south of Louisa County, to the town of Richmond and its Courthouse along the Yadkin River near East Bend. In time, he purchased more land, which indicates that he was rather well to do.

Strange quirks of fate have become woven into the Poindexter family stories. When the railroad came through, the selection of a name for the station to be built in what was "Bailie Bottoms" was given to Dr. Samuel Martin, great grandson of Elizabeth "Betty" Pledge Poindexter. It was to be named for Chief Donnahoo, but it was mis-spelled and became Donnaha Station. Now it's just Donnaha, a siding.

In another twist, before the county lines were redrawn, Richmond Courthouse was the County Seat for Surry County. It was in the town known locally as "Old Richmond." Thomas Poindexter owned lots 9 and 10 in the town, costing a total of four dollars. He must have had interest in a hotel because Betty Pledge Poindexter ran a hotel in Richmond prior to 1830, and Andrew Jackson, later to become President of the United States, overnighted there once as a young man. A short time later, the town was obliterated by a tornado and nothing is left to this day.

In another case, settling up the estate after Thomas Jr. died, a portion of "Bailie Bottoms" was sectioned off to become the "Carson Tract" and lost some of its identity. And, one of Thomas' sons, Robert Alexander, was a noted horseman who acquired fine stock from Kentucky. He raced his horses on a well known track in "Bailie Bottoms." It's gone, too.

102

Were it not for the Railroad, Donnaha and all reference to our Indian heritage in these lands would be lost.

When the Revolution came along, Thomas, Jr. was an ardent Patriot and held the rank of Captain. He commanded a company of North Carolina Militia with the North Carolina Revolutionary Army. By then he and his wife had children, and a young daughter, Ann, is recorded to have taken messages sewn into her petticoat through British lines, thus becoming a spy and subject to execution if caught, along with the entire Poindexter family. Those must have been trying times of great worry, but for an enthralled little girl listening to stories, they were very exciting to me.

After the war, Thomas Poindexter became a planter of means and acquired large land grants in what was Rowan County, now Surry and Yadkin Counties because the County lines have changed since then. He died on January 1, 1807. His wife died on February 1816, and both of them lie buried on a bluff overlooking the Yadkin River.

Their next to last child, Robert Alexander, was called "Blaze" because of his temper. In addition to horses, he was also a fine musician who taught anyone who was interested to sing, children and neighbors alike. His second wife was the subject of a fine story.

It seems that she first married Benjamin Pettitt on May 12, 1819, and they relocated to the Holston River valley in eastern Tennessee. That was particularly wild country at the time, and her husband soon died leaving her with a small child and a twelve year old brother alone in a log cabin. One night, while drying out fat provided by a neighbor who had killed hogs for her, bears came about the place and were at her door. She pushed furniture up against the door, and with her baby in her arms, she and her brother climbed the chimney for safety. Recognizing that the hot fire kept the bears out, she kept the fire stoked all night. With the dawn and with the bear threat subsided, she was finished with frontier life, and the three of them rode a mule back home. They rode for days through Indian country where more bears roamed. They crossed river and mountain alike, finally making it home.

Robert Alexander must have liked her spirit. He came by one day while she was washing clothes and proposed on the spot. She accepted, left her wash tub, and they were married that day. They had ten children.

Now, back to my line.

Capt. Thomas Poindexter's son, John, their eighth of twelve children, married Sarah James. Their daughter, Patsy, married Austin Trulove. Their daughter, Mary Martha Trulove, married Bennett Martin, and that started my Poindexter-to-Martin line. And for certain, another set of stories of war.

Bennett Martin was killed on May 23, 1864 during the Battle of Hanover Junction near Richmond, Virginia. It seems that Private Martin had been enlisted at East Bend on the first day of February, 1863, and served in the 28th Regiment of North Carolina Confederate Army. A Lieutenant in the Confederate Army, J. G. Trulove, a relative, enlisted him for the duration of the war. Bennett didn't come home. He's buried somewhere in Virginia and served all of his time during the war without pay. His wife, Mary Millinder, applied for his compensation and received nothing. Her son, John Martin, said that she died of a broken heart at thirty-one years of age having lost everything to the Civil War.

Bennett left three sons. One, Alexander Wesley

Martin, was my Grandfather. He didn't like the sound of his name and reversed it to Wesley Alexander. Mr. W. A. Martin, along with his house and store in East Bend, were my mother's home place where I often visited with her from our home in Little Richmond. I knew him as Mr. W. A. Martin and thought I had named one of my sons, William Alexander, after him, but I learned later that his name was Wesley Alexander. The Wesley connection was carried on by my son when he gave his second son that name. He is now a medical doctor. In fact, both of Alex's sons, Squire and Wesley, are medical doctors.

Another interesting bit concerns my teeth. There wasn't a dentist anywhere around Little Richmond, so one of the reasons that Mama used to visit East Bend when I was a little girl was to have my teeth looked after. Right there in the middle of East Bend, in one of its second story offices, Rosebud Morse Garriet had hung out her shingle. She was the first woman dentist in North Carolina, but how she came to that profession and why she ended up in East Bend, I don't know.

Nearby, on the "Bailie Bottoms" area was where Saura Town once existed. It was populated by the Saura Indians, and so far as I know, Saura Town Mountains is the only reference to them that remains in the land that they once inhabited. They lived in bark houses and must have carried on extensive trade and travel. The Yadkin was, no doubt, a major highway for them that went all the way to the coast. The Saura were not Cherokee. They didn't have the same characteristics at all like the Cherokee. The Cherokee were a much browner people and had a different appearance. So, I suspect that the Saura were much easier to assimilate into the blood lines of the white settlers that came into North Carolina, and that was how they vanished.

There were four different types of Indians here at the time white settlers came to North Carolina. This colony was in the hands of the Lords Proprietors in England, land speculators, who were seeking their fortunes, and unlike Virginia, North Carolina was not a Royal Colony with all the privileges thereunto. So, people poured into North Carolina from all over Europe and pushed the Indians westward. The Tuscarora Indian war down on the coast around New Bern was a particularly nasty massacre, for example. The Indians that lived down along the coast spoke a language similar to the Indians in what became New York State. On the other end of North Carolina, in the mountains, were the Cherokee. In the middle were those known as Saura and Lumbee, and who knows what else.

According to old timers in the area, the Indians called Pilot Mountain "Jomeokee." Since it stood out for miles, and still does, it was their landmark for traveling up and down the river and throughout this area. The Indians traveling east to west, and the other way, too, when coming to Jomeokee, they knew where they were. One of the major Indian routes running north-to-south went straight south toward Charlotte, and they kept Jomeokee on their left. Charlotte is built on the junction of two big Indian trails. Where Tryon and Trade Streets cross, the very center of Charlotte, is where those trails crossed. There used to be a huge old oak tree there that the city valued, and they tried to keep it alive, but it died of great age taking away another of the Indian landmarks in our region.

I remember that when Rosebud worked on my teeth, she told me that I had Indian blood because of the formation of my upper incisors. She said that anybody that came out of Indian stock had teeth like mine. So, I suppose that a few clues are left if you know where to look and what to look for. I suspect that lots of Saura Indian blood flows through the hearts of many North Carolinians around East Bend and the Yadkin River valley, and the only indicator is likely to be in their teeth.

East Bend by way of Donnaha and the railroad was where Mama and I were headed when I first started this tale. We would go visit Grandma Flora, my mother's Mama, and all of Mama's sisters our family in that area. Flora was the daughter of John H. Poindexter, named Flora Anna. She was from the long line of Poindexters all the way back to the Isle of Jersey as I mentioned earlier. And along the way we incorporated American Indian stock to become who we are.

Games & Money

Lucille and me, 1925
Dresses by Florence Carter

When children got together on the school yard, one of the games that everybody could take part in was playing "crack the whip." Everyone held hands in a long line, and the object was for the person at the head of the line to give a great tug and pull the line toward him so that everyone had to run madly toward him to keep from being separated. Whoever was at the end of the line would, sometimes, get thrown quite a distance. That was the fun part, seeing who was thrown the farthest.

A game of ball we played was "Ante Over." I have no idea where the name came from, or if that's the correct name. Anyway, two groups of children would gather on either side of a building, and a ball would be thrown over preceded by the receiving side yelling "Ante." The throwing side would yell "over," and over would come the ball. The object was to see which side could catch the ball and throw it back over the quickest and farthest so that those on the opposite side had to back up to the point that they could no longer throw the ball over the building. The side that won mostly padded its team with the biggest boys with the strongest arms. The ball was usually a homemade baseball, a tight ball of twine.

We didn't have any equipment for playing games, so one of our favorites was called "kick the can." It required only an old can, usually a one gallon size such as a paint can. One of us would be "It," and the object was that everyone else would hide as "It" counted to twenty. "It" hid his face, then would try to discover someone in hiding and run back to the can and kick it before the person in hiding got there, thus shifting "It" to the new person. What made the game fun was that while "It" had his back turned searching for hiders, anyone in hiding could run out and kick the can sending it who knows where. "It" would then have to find the can and kick it back to where he thought it would be to his advantage and begin again trying to find hiders, but he couldn't get too far from the can. "It" would sometimes become quite exasperated, especially if the game was played after dark and the hiders could run faster and get to the can before him. The object was to run from hiding to the can before "It" so that you were "home free" and removed from the game a winner by not becoming "It."

The bigger boys particularly liked "kick the can" because they could run fast and kick the can the farthest, much to "Its" displeasure. With a new "It" determined by counting out, the game started over again. Since the can was always kicked far from him, "It" had a hard time in this game. Nobody wanted to be "It," and the smallest child that always wanted to play with the bigger children would end up in tears because he couldn't catch anyone.

During the winter there wasn't much to do but sit around the fire trying to keep warm. Most people had open fireplaces because there weren't many stoves in our area of the country. Every fireplace had one of those little wire baskets for popping pop corn over hot coals. All that was required was your popper, pop corn, a dish pan, and a salt shaker. People strung their ears of pop corn up to dry in the attic, or someplace in the house, and once it was popped a couple of little ears would fill a dish pan. We didn't put anything on it but salt, and we would sit around the fire and tell tales while eating our popcorn. Daddy told all sorts of long, drawn out tales about what he used to do when he was on the road as a traveling salesman.

When I visited with my friend Mattie Ruth Wilmoth, we played with the out-of-date Sears and Roebuck catalog. We'd cut pictures out of the catalog and assemble families. We'd have a father and a mother and several children, and we'd name them all and dress them with what we found in the catalog. Our play area was divided into "Your House" and "My House," and we would play bringing our families over to visit. We'd happily fill a whole afternoon, if we had that much time.

In the summertime, we would construct very imaginary play houses. When the older folks were working around a tobacco barn stringing up tobacco, us children got the tag ends of the tobacco twine and tied them up to make walls from one tree to another. We'd leave an opening for a door, and outline things in our houses with stones. We'd find moss and fix green beds covered with the softest and best moss we could find. We'd save every bottle cap and jar lid we could find; they made very good pie pans and table ware. A flat rock became our table, and we'd make mud pies and serve dinners and go through all the merigamaroll imitating life as we knew it.

Tobacco worms provided endless entertainment. We'd have races with them, sometimes on the ground on tracks we made or along twine strung as an high wire act. We'd tie one end of a piece of twine to a pole and the other end below it tightly to another pole. That would be one race track. Beside it we'd make another one and so on for everyone who wanted to race. Each of us would get a big, fat worm and put them at the top end of the track and see which one would win by climbing down the string to the other end. We provided a lot of encouragement to our racers by screaming and hollering for our particular worm.

Children, boys and girls, had to use their imaginations back then. There wasn't much that was bought from stores. A nice chip of wood could make a fine car. A line of white stones made a perfectly acceptable wall. A little string and an active imagination built an entire house. We could play for hours and hours and be the most contented children you've ever seen.

How little boys played? When Ben was little... he was so enamored with cars, but we didn't see many of them. That was in the early 1930s. We lived in sight of the new sand clay road that rerouted the main road to Elkin from in front of Daddy's house to a new route along the ridge and down the hill to Burch Station. There were eight years difference in our ages, and I baby-sat Ben when he was in diapers. When Mama went to the garden, I had to mind the baby. After Ben got bigger, he and a little colored boy named Wylie Cockerham, who lived on the place, played together for hours and hours. If they heard a car growling along in low gear coming up the steep Burch hill, they would run up the road and get just as close to the highway as they could to see the car go by. One night at the supper table, Ben was just as proud as punch and said, "I saw THREE cars today!"

He and Wylie were always making little cars. They would take the tag ends sawed off a plank and shape them into cars. They'd have wheels, and all the black shoe polish would get gone.

Mama couldn't keep black shoe polish in the house. Sunday would come, and we'd need to polish our shoes. Well, there wouldn't be a bottle on the place. Mama would say, "I know I bought a bottle of shoe polish. Now where did I put it?"

Ben and Wylie always had the nicest, shiny, little black cars you've ever seen. There was a big sand pile down on the hill behind the house, and they had built an entire race track in it. Up, down, and around the track they went, playing hour by hour by hour, making racing sounds and just having the best time.

I never had any association with big boys, so I don't know what bigger boys did for play. Children were kept pretty close to home, especially the girls.

Wylie was one of the children of the first colored family to live on our place. Mr. Cocherham was a widower with two children. The girl was older and the boy was younger. That was Wylie. They made out with a tobacco barn that Daddy converted for them to live in. Times were tougher for some folks, and the rest of us did what we could to help. Daddy had the poles cut out of the barn and built a rock and mud chimney onto it, and he had a kitchen and a sitting room with a porch built onto the east side of the barn. A door up some steps led into the kitchen, and from there a door to the right led to a sitting room before going into the barn portion of the house. It wasn't a fine house by any means, but it was substantial enough for several families who needed a helping hand along the way.

They stayed with us several years, five, six, seven maybe, and moved away, and we lost track of them. Years later, a colored man came and knocked on my door. It was Wylie; he was trying to find out about Ben. They had moved to Chicago, and he had made a barber. He was in the area visiting his Cockerham relatives and came to see about Ben. After all those years, he was looking for his boyhood pal.

There were two families of Cockerhams in our area, Quiller and his brother who lived up the road on the Mt. Hermon Church road. I think the two of them accounted for twenty-five or twenty-six children between them. They were smart people, hard working. Quiller's brother had the land adjacent to Daddy's Yadkin River bottom farm.

Quiller was handy at about anything anybody might want to build, and his wife, Effie, rode to work with me eight or ten years. She used to tend to Sam Gentry's children when they were little, and she rode with me every day to Dobson and back. I thought the world of Effie. We were all very comfortable together.

Wylie's father was named Harrison. He had a brother named Wash Cockerham, maybe short for Washington. After Harrison and his two children left our farm, they moved over onto Dock Ashburn's farm above Snow Creek down toward the Mitchell River. Wash Cockerham lived on the place for, maybe, six years after that. That's where the daughter died, and we lost track of them when the men moved away.

When I was a little girl, when we went to Dock Ashburn's, we'd go down behind the barn, cross the branch, and follow the path through the woods and come out at Dock's corn field right in his back yard. The river road that ran along the east bank of the Mitchell went right in front of their house and on up to the Joe Layne's Mill road. They were good people, Molly and Dock. They never learned to read or write, and when they had need of such services, we would provide.

The place belonged to Molly. She was an "old maid" who had spent her youth taking care of her parents who had gotten so old that they were past doing for themselves. She had to plough and chop the wood and do all the work. Dock was an old bachelor who lived farther down the hill toward the Mitchell, and he would pass the place from time to time. He knew her predicament, and one day he lingered at the wood pile while she wrestled with a log, and he very quietly said to her, "I'll chop your wood if you'll make my

114

bread." She looked at him and saw that he meant it, so they were married. Both of them were too old to have children, but he helped her care for her folks until their passing.

The Ashburn house was a log cabin with one main room and walls papered with newspaper. A lean-to kitchen was built onto the back. Molly and Dock always kept guineas, they were better at telling strangers were in the yard than a dog. Dock had a big whetstone that turned with a hand crank in the front yard under a tree. He could put an edge on a axe that would shave a man.

Molly, Opal White and Dock Ashburn at their home on the Mitchell River c. 1938

The place came to Molly, and Dock never had to work to accumulate money to buy land. When they came to the age to be concerned about their future, they got my parents to write Molly's will. It was a good thing they did. They had taken a girl named Opal to raise. She was orphaned in a big family; her father was left without a wife with four little girls. Molly said she'd take Opal. All the girls

115

found homes, and as time passed, Molly wanted to leave her land to Opal. So, Mama and Daddy wrote her will. In time, Molly passed on, and a few years later, Dock followed. By then some of Dock's people were watching things mighty closely, and went to the law trying to take the property away from Opal. Mama and Daddy went to court to support Opal's claim and told how they wrote the will. So, the Ashburn heirs were not able to break the will. Opal married Tom Brown, and they lived on the place for a while, but they wanted to get work off the farm, so Opal sold the property and bought a place in Dobson for them.

Yards. Molly stooped to cut another plant for her home pharmacy, adding to her basket already full. Nothing she liked better than a ramble in the woods and field. Years of family recipes were stored in her head - she could not read or write, nor felt the need to.

Off the road in quiet woods, her house bespoke mountain construction: logs, added frame kitchen, and rock chimney. Molly still cooked on the fireplace although a shiny wood fired range stood ready.

"Mostly, I kindle the range for bread," she said, "but bilin' goes in the firepot." And she'd smile, broken-toothed. All of us Martin children loved to visit Molly and eat delicious food cooked from that black pot. It hung on an iron crane that swung out of the fireplace. And sweet potatoes baked in the ashes; good memories of childhood.

Dock was a good man, just a country farmer. I

remember once when I was about twelve years old, I stuck a nail in my foot. You didn't go to the doctor for everything back then. It was during cherry picking time, and Mama was busy with canning cherries. There was a long row of cherry trees down the ridge here, and people would come and pick them on halves. Mama thought she had to can every one of her half, and she did the best she could with my sore foot, but it wasn't getting a bit better. I kept it elevated, propped on pillows, and it swelled to twice the normal size with big red streaks coming up my leg to the knee. I was in dreadful pain. Something had to be done.

Dock heard that something was the matter with my foot, and he came in the house one day and asked to look at my wound. I was in bed. He tutted his tongue a few times and went out and gathered up a great bundle of stinking jimpson weed, ugly, bad smelling stuff. He got Mama's biggest biscuit pan and filled it with the dark green leaves, then put the pan in the oven. While the leaves heated, he took away the pillows and spread newspapers in a thick pad under my foot. When the leaves were wilted and hot, he packed them around my foot and wrapped everything in a piece of old blanket.

"Now," he told Mama. "Keep up the fire."

He went out and gathered more leaves. All day the relays went on; hot leaves, replaced as soon as they cooled, with a fresh, hot poultice. At early lamplight, Dock pointed to a small river of green pus draining from the puncture. Eventually, the place broke open and drained, and the red streaks up my leg went away.

That was my first blood poisoning. Back then when you got sick, you either got better or you didn't. It was as simple as that, and Dock had taken care of one that would

probably have been a "didn't get better" for me.
Infections were dreaded before sulfa drugs and penicillin. Dock and Molly were herbalists. They were in demand among the neighbors all around.
There was some business in herbal medicine. Ginseng root, called "sang," brought a good price. It was purchased by S. V. Tomlinson's in North Wilkesboro.
Molly made tea of dogwood bark for ague (contains quinine); of willow bark for pain (contained salicin); of clover to strengthen the heart; of senna for laxative. For antiseptic, she infused marigold petals. Powdered geranium root was good for wounds.

"Lore," we call it now; it was the means of treatment for all the ills flesh is heir to throughout the centuries. Much has been lost; some is being reclaimed as herbal medicine seems to be receiving growing interest nowadays.
It was amazing what uses liquor had. There was nothing better for an infant who had colic and couldn't sleep. You took a little bit of boiled water and sweetened it, then put one drop of mountain dew in it and fed it to the baby. And, oh, it would sleep like a lamb. When a child got a little older and got "the croup," everybody knew that you melted your hard candy, rock candy or horehound, and added your mountain dew to it. If you had a lemon you squeezed a little into it, and you made an excellent cough syrup.
If you were caught out in the weather and you got

wet and it was a while before you could get dry, you were apt to get a chill. It was just as important to get warmed on the inside as it was on the outside, and a nip would do the job pretty well. Otherwise, you might take pneumonia. In those days, pneumonia was a nine day thing until the fever broke or you died. Nursing was what kept people alive; there weren't any antibiotics.

If you had trouble getting off to sleep, a good way to help was to have a dram at bedtime. A nip was from the bottle, and dram was from the glass. Womenfolk would never drink from the bottle; it wasn't ladylike, you see.

Any little country store had a small stock of home remedies. I remember that there were little bottles of gum camphor. You would dissolve gum camphor in mountain dew, and it made a wonderful liniment if you had a muscle ache.

For the older people who didn't stir around much and complained of poor circulation, there was nothing better than a little mountain dew as a regular treatment. When people became bed-ridden, everyone knew that bed sores resulted, on their hips, on their backs, where their bones were close to the skin, and the best cure known for bed sores was to go to the druggist and get bismuth subcarbonate, add liquor to it a drop at a time until you worked up a paste, then apply the paste to the bed sores. It worked.

Of course there were people who over-indulged, and others would try to get them to take the pledge to put their evil habits behind them. Mama used to tell a funny story about a woman in East Bend who was married to a drunkard. He wouldn't work, and he provided children with regularity but nothing to support them. The poor woman was reduced to taking in washing and grubbing in a garden to grow vegetables for her children, and her husband wouldn't hit a lick. When the preacher came to see her, he saw how hard this woman was having to work, and he tried to pray with the husband and change his way, but all efforts never changed a thing. So finally, the preacher and his congregation resorted to reverse psychology; they took up an offering and bought a whole keg of liquor, legal liquor, and delivered it to the house. The spokesman said to the husband, "We've decided that we're not going to waste any more time trying to persuade you to do the right thing. We have a great respect and sympathy for your poor wife, so we have taken up a collection to buy this whiskey for you. And we want you to drink yourself to death just as quickly as you can, so this poor woman will be rid of you." Well, it made the man so mad that he straightened up and quit drinking.

One way a young person could make a little money back then was by selling seeds. Certain seed companies would advertise that if you wanted to sell seeds for them, they would provide a box of different kinds of seeds likely to be of interest in your area, mostly vegetables and flowers, and all you did was sell the seeds for the price printed on their packages. You sent most of the money back to the company and got to keep a little for yourself.

Another way to get things that was popular was selling Cloverine Salve. It came in round metal containers and was used for all kinds of skin irritations, skinned knees, open places and the like. If you bought a can of Cloverine Salve you got a beautiful picture, usually of the Savior or the two little children on the precipice with a winged angel spread above them. They were hung in homes throughout this part of the country.

Women accumulated various size glasses and goblets with their snuff purchases. They would trade with each other to make whatever set they were trying to put together. Glassware also came in oatmeal cans and other consumables that were incentives for housewives to purchase these products. I still have oatmeal glasses, and a cream and sugar set that's no telling how old. I can remember when people bought their gasoline at places that gave away dishes as an incentive to buy their gasoline.

Table glasses also came with jelly. Mama made her own jelly, but she bought enough for a set of glasses that Michaela still has.

Business was done everywhere. When you went to church, on the backs of the pews were racks to hold the hymn books. Everybody knows that, but also in the rack you were likely to find paper fans with stapled on stick handles. The fans were advertisements for dry goods stores, all kinds of area establishments, even undertakers. Those fans were put to good use on hot summer days when the churches got stuffy with heat. I suspect that they generated some business for the ladies who remembered the cooling breezes those fans provided.

And feed sacks. Lordy, everybody who got their feed in sacks got to pick the pattern they wanted for a new dress. It was good, substantial cloth, and on Sunday morning, a well made feed sack dress was in fine company. If you knew your feed sack patterns, you could identify who was wearing what, but it didn't matter. Everyone was in the same boat doing whatever they had to do to get along without money. If the sack material was starched and ironed, it finished as pretty as linen. Of course, everything had to be ironed on those days. Everything wrinkled so badly.

I'm afraid that the children were less kind about feed sack dresses, though. They knew what feed sack material looked like, too. All the little girls were prim and proper in their dresses regardless of where they came from, but those among them who had store bought or tailor made dresses could make a little girl feel awfully bad about her feed sack dress. Nothing was wasted, though.

When I was a little girl, on Sundays when we went to Church in Salem Fork, Aunt Bessie, Tom's wife, would let us children play in the old store. It still had a few pairs of those high-topped shoes with spool heels, several old hats, this and that, along with rolls of gauze that they used to cover tobacco plant beds in the spring. She gave us short lengths of this cloth, and we would braid it into big rolls of "hair." We'd dress up with the shoes and hats we found and have the biggest time.

There was a pair of black leather high tops with high heels and at least two dozen tiny buttons up the front. Ladies used special button hooks to button up their shoes in those days, and with things like that we would strut around the finest of ladies.

Oh! That was more fun than anything I did in my

life. We all had high society names; I remember Hazel's, their daughter who was about my age. Hers was Hewzey Stegal, maybe it was Stigall. Irene was Mrs. Masten. Lora was Mrs. Hubbard, and I think Joyce was Hallie Graatz, or something like that. After we got all doodied up, we would see which one of us could tell the biggest lies about our families, such as how many children we had, and what size house we lived in.

Then, we would go for walks, strutting about, you see: the high society life. One time all dressed up like that, we were walking down the road and met Uncle Newt. He pretended that he didn't know us.

"Good evening, ladies," he said. "How are you this fine evening?"

I think it was Irene who asked him the way to Ester Moser's house, and he just played along making it so much fun for us. They were all so good to children in that family, and even though he had no children, Newt could play along with the best of us.

It was along about then that the younger of Tom's children, Ray and Lora, got a little goat. They named it Nanny Butts. Nanny was supposed to live in the barn, but she was sort of free to run around the yard. Well, Nanny Butts was a smart animal who wanted more than anything to be with the children. She learned how to open the front door, and everyone soon had to watch out for her because she would come right on in the house and climb right on up the stairs where the children slept.

Well, after a while of Nanny Butts becoming part of the family, Newt had bought some high powered fertilizer and had an open bag of it out at the barn. Nanny got into it, and when they found the little goat, she was stretched out ready to die, just blowing tiny bubbles, barely breathing.

Newt was tore up about what had happened to Nanny Butts and was all but wringing his hands over the poor thing. All of the children gathered around and got down on their knees and prayed and prayed and carried on for the goat. But Nanny Butts just laid there; such a pitiful sight.

And, do you know, after a while, Nanny Butts got up and was soon her old self again. We were all so happy to have Nanny Butts back again.

After that, everyone was careful to fasten up all the bags of stuff around the barn that Nanny Butts might get into.

Life Behind the Potted Plant

I finished high school in the spring of 1935 and started college in the fall. I was the valedictorian and gave the little speech before the assembled proceedings. They gave me a small gold pin, which I lost two or three years down the road.

I suppose that, for the times, you could say that Dobson High School was a small school. I believe the head count was twenty-eight, maybe thirty, in the graduating class. I remember the count that was made when our 50th Reunion was held, but we had lost a number of our class-mates by then. Most interestingly, we had lost nearly

Wintertime school days, Dobson, North Carolina c. 1934

all of our basketball players, a top notch basketball team, State Champions. Dobson was, I believe, State Champions two years running. It was quite a successful team, but all of them didn't live to make old bones.

In terms of what we could do in school, we all did more or less the same things; we didn't have very much choice in those days. There was English, required. I did French - not everybody did foreign language. The girls did Home Economics; the boys did shop. We had algebra and geometry, one year of each. Civics was in there, a course on government. We weren't terribly well educated, but we were supposed to know something about each of the basics of education. We didn't have much as extra-curricular activities because over half the class rode busses in and out of school from way out in the county, and not very many people had vehicles then; country people couldn't be taking their children to school things all the time. There was too much work to do.

126

I met the school bus on the sand clay road every morning, Route 268 had not been numbered at the time, and, of course, I rode it home every afternoon. The bus went on down the hill, by Burch Station, across the Mitchell River, and on up 268 to the road by Friendship Church. It made the circle by the church, came back down the CCC Camp road back to the river and on to Dobson. That was a long route, and it took a lot of time. The students on the west side of the river helped build up the size of Dobson High School a little.

The sand clay road, later numbered Route 268, was built as a dirt road about 1924 or '25. I remember that they had very little machinery; the workers used mules to pull the drags, and they plowed up the bed for the road and did a lot of hauling. They used manpower mostly in those days. Now you see men standing around and machines doing the work. Up through 1935 when I went off to college, the road stayed pretty much the same. It wasn't hard-surfaced for several more years.

Daddy had decided that he wanted his girls to learn to play the piano. So, he bought one and had it moved into the front room of our house here; a big upright that sat in the same place for many, many years. My piano teacher got on the train once a week and came down from Ronda to Burch Station. Lucille and I had the same teacher. I was between eight and nine; Lucille was a little younger. By the time I was twelve I was playing in the churches around here. You really didn't have to be too proficient; if people could recognize the tune, that was good enough.

There wasn't any music to speak of in school, there was some art, but mostly what we did was on our own. We did a few water colors, a little drawing, nothing to crow about. Anyhow, one year Mama took one of my pictures to the Elkin Fair. I was about twelve. It won a prize; a three week pass to the Lyric Theater in Elkin.

Ohhh! Did my eyes light up, but she told me, "We can't take you to the picture show, and we don't approve of them, anyway. So, I sold it for three dollars. Now, here's the three dollars. Go put it in the bank."

So, I did, and the bank went broke; lost my three dollars and the gold money piece I'd won for spelling. I remember when all the banks around closed their doors, and these poor tobacco farmers around here... they'd raised a big crop, took it to Winston-Salem, sold it and didn't have much left. I heard one say that after paying his hauling bill, he had enough left to buy a pair of overshoes for his whole load of tobacco, practically a season's work.

It was hard times then. In some ways I had more advantages than most everyone else in the country around here. I remember that we didn't have electric lights, but Daddy bought one of those Aladdin lanterns that had a globe that gave off a nice bright light. It was put on the big walnut table in the dining room for us to study by. Lucille, Ben and I did our studying around that lantern. We had a piano with instruction, and I got to read the school teacher's magazines. We had boarders then, and I thought there was nothing in the world as wonderful as Redbook, Cosmopolitan, and Saturday Evening Post because they were running wonderful stories in installments by Willa Cather and all those great writers.

During that time, I was nine, ten, eleven, twelve, I could read anything for pleasure. I could take a telephone book when I was out of reading material and just entertain myself in the best fashion. Ever since, print and I have been

128

best of friends. Later on, when I was in college, I was able to make a little money by reading.

I played piano for my class in school, for singing and for the occasional program. I remember that I played for the graduating class, my own class, when we were graduated from the eighth grade. I was often at the keyboard. Music wasn't taught in the school; it was all private. One year, one of my teachers, Mrs. Stanley, got up a little chorus; they had a singing when all the choruses showed up over at the Franklin School at White Plains. That was all there was for music in school when I came along.

One year there was a debating society, and at first, it competed just in the county. Our team at Dobson won and got to go to Chapel Hill for the next round, the state level. I was part of the team, but we got whipped. We made the first round, then a team smarter than us cut us down.

I wound up at Berea College because there was no question about applying to an expensive school. Daddy, in calling on the merchants in Wilkes County, got into conversation with a man named Bryan and found out that his daughter had graduated from Berea College and was currently a teacher in the area. He told Daddy that Berea had nothing like the expenses of the colleges in North Carolina, and it had a work program for the students. Daddy asked them to get the addresses and application blanks for me, and Miss Vera Bryan sent all this material. In the spring I took it up to the High School in Dobson, and they proctored it - let me take the examination - and when it was finished I sent it in.

You had to be pretty high in your class to be considered at all for entrance into Berea College, and at the top, I was rated high enough. But they wrote and asked if I really wanted to start college at the age of sixteen, that's pretty young. Didn't I want to wait a year?

I wrote back and asked what would I do during the year I was waiting; I would forget a lot of high school. I'd rather start and go. So, they said OK, and along with all the other freshmen, I arrived in Berea to go to college that fall.

I'd never been anywhere much. Lois Folger, from my class at Dobson, also went to Berea. We were room mates our first year, in Kentucky Hall. The two of us traveled by Greyhound Bus to Knoxville where we had a layover of about four hours, and then we went the rest of the trip, also by bus. We were met by upperclassmen, and they had three or four days to help get all of us freshmen settled in before going off to their classes while we started ours.

That's me, college girl, 1936

All the freshmen girls had to wash dishes in boarding school. After meals, we'd stack dishes while the boys brought pans of hot water to the tables. Then we'd wash and rinse and stack, ready for the next meal. And then the boys would empty the water; we'd clean up until the next meal. That was one of the little jobs that paid my way for college.

We had other jobs available to us. I worked in the candy kitchen for a while, that was just one of the college's industries. Then, I went over to the Boone Tavern. I heard that sometimes, at mid-term, they would take on some extra hands. So, they took me on, and I waited tables there.

Everything in my classes was very enjoyable, except chemistry. I made the lowest grade I made in my entire life, and it didn't worry me a bit. I saw that it wasn't for me. I'd go to lab, and I'd get up on my stool, look around and see what everyone else was doing, open a book and sit there and read. I actually did diddlely-squat and got a "D." It should have been an "F" I suspect, but in everything else I did very well. Of course, I was doing piano.

Who knows what my ambition was in going to Berea College? I'm not really sure what I was after. I was fairly proficient with piano from private lessons, and I had picked up more and went on from there. I had already put in two or three years of playing for the Baptist Church here in Little Richmond, then on Preaching Sundays, I'd play the organ, a pump organ. So, for hymns and other sorts of community music, I was rather accomplished as a young girl. Finding my way, I suppose.

After I went to work at Boone Tavern, there were two ladies who were residents there, a mother and her old maid daughter. The mother was a little petite thing with curly hair and always so fashionably dressed. The daughter was so plain, and she didn't see very well. In conversation, she mentioned that she was looking for someone to read to her, and I told her I would. So, she'd get her books out of the library, and on pleasant days we'd walk out on campus

131

and find a sunny bench.

You try reading George Santayana aloud to somebody, or the Mississippi writer, Faulkner, with his mythical Yoknapatawpha County.... Some of his sentences are half a page long. Oh, the breath required.

And while I was in college, I sang in the Sunday Morning choir. You had a choice of starving on Sunday morning, sleeping to just time to run to the church service, or we could get up at six thirty and go to the boarding hall to eat whatever they served on Sunday mornings, a cooked cereal - cream of wheat, no doubt; milk, bread and butter; a damson plum, sliced peaches; juice. All of it came from the college kitchens, creamery, bakery, orchards.... That's the way the college made it through, along with student workers to support their education.

I would starve in order to sleep, then rush around and run in the back door of the church, run up the corkscrew staircase to the level where the choir robed and came out into the loft. I was an alto in the second row, and just about the time I settled down and everything would get quiet, my stomach would cut loose. Ohhh! I would clinch my stomach; I would draw up. Well, nothing kept the starving noises from their duties, and I would swear to myself that next Sunday I would get up early enough to eat breakfast. I would not let this happen again. But, it always did.

College life was going to class, work, and lots more little things like seeing to your own laundry. Berea College had a lovely library - books, books, books. We were required to do a certain amount of group exercises over at Seabury Gym, and I began to play for the folk dancing groups. I did a summer school with them between my freshman and sophomore years, playing for folk dancing. Mr. Smith, who lived up on the hill above Dr. Gabbard's house, the dentist, taught a lot of them. I took some other courses that had to do with music, courses like sight reading, harmony, orchestral technique, those sorts of things to help me learn more.

After supper we could sign out. There were hours we were supposed to keep when we were supposed to be in the dorm, but if we needed to go somewhere, the library for instance, we could sign out, go over there and do whatever was needed. We were required to be in at a certain time, and like everything else, we were required to go to chapel just about every day.

We had some interesting speakers at chapel, and musicians especially. I recall this lovely Russian quartet who were on tour, four men - not one of them under three hundred pounds; a basso that could just curl your toenails he could sing so low. They sang in Russian, beautiful songs. There were various writers who talked about their work and where they came from; poetry readings.

Most every day the college had something like this, and attendance was checked, so you had to be there. We had assigned seating and someone went around with a book recording who was and wasn't there. We were shown a little of everything, even movies. There wasn't a theater on campus; they used the chapel with its stage in the round, horseshoe seating around it and the balcony. They would drop a screen for the occasional movie showing.

Beyond that, I didn't know anything about life in Berea. I was an ignorant little country girl; I was comfortable with books but I was awkward with people, and I never had much social life while growing up here in Little

Richmond because if you are set down at an early age behind a piano and a potted plant, that's your life from then on. Other people dance, other people sing, and from behind the potted plant you make the music that other people socialize to. That's what I knew.

Winters in college were about like winters ought to be. We had to wear boots and heavy coats to keep warm, but the college had a good grounds crew who kept the

Berea College, classes and more c. 1954. It's chimes were heard throughout Berea.

sidewalks clear, and the buildings were warm. During the spring and fall, the weather was usually nice for extended periods of time, and the one summer I worked at Boone Tavern, after my freshman year, I found Kentucky summers to be about what I had been accustomed to growing up in North Carolina.

That summer I did a few other things to keep busy, waiting tables, folk music, reading, and I walked a little girl. Her people wanted to get her out in the fresh air and to get some exercise, so we walked around the main part of town and the campus talking and looking at whatever we came across. In quiet moments, I could always get a book and settle down in a corner somewhere. So, I didn't socialize much.

I did two years at Berea, then married Taylor Price Gabbard during the summer after my second year. It was 1937. I did a little of everything while I was in college at Berea; I did a little sewing, not too much while I was in school, but after I was married I began sewing rather quickly because we couldn't afford to buy children's clothes and Taylor was such a big man it was hard to find clothes his size. One way and another, I did a lot of sewing then.

Tailoring for women was a way to make some money that we sorely needed. Clients would supply the pattern and fabric, then seemed to always drop by at supper time for fitting. A lady's suit brought five dollars, and that much money could go a long way. I did my sewing after my children were in bed, meaning that I didn't get much sleep working long hours at night tailoring.

I was gone from Berea College for several years, raising a family, then after I discovered that I needed to finish college in order to teach, I started again. By then, we had gone our separate ways, and I taught on a "C" (emergency) Certificate in 1950 and '51 in North Carolina; that was because I was among friends here. There were no teaching jobs with that kind of certificate in Kentucky.

When I went back to Berea, in 1952 and '53, I'd been out of school so long that courses and requirements had changed. I'd never had any humanities, although I had taken Latin, but they arranged for me to quality for Foreign

135

Language credit by taking the French test without classes. I just read for it, took the test, and passed it.

By then, I had read anything I could get my hands on. I was fortunate that, sometimes, it was a big help to me. I had a book of French short stories written in English and very nearly knew each one by heart. Down the road, when I came to qualify for my Bachelor of Arts degree several years later, the second time I was at Berea College, I was told that, since I had two year's credit in Latin for college and French in high school, if I passed the language exam, it would complete my requirements. So, I got The Count of Monte Cristo and the Bible in French, and as time permitted, when I wasn't studying something else or wiping children's noses or cooking, I would do what reading I could. The exam was in two parts, the first with a dictionary, timed and proctored. The second was read from French to be rendered into English without a dictionary, and also in an allotted amount of time.

Well, I read the first sentence or two and recognized that it was from my book of famous French stories, one about Crankabille, the vegetable monger, who pushed his cart through the city streets selling to whomever wanted his produce. The housewives would call down to him from windows above, then run out into the street and pay him for what they wanted. One of them kept him and kept him while she looked over his produce, then he had to wait as she went back into her house to get the money to pay him. Along came a policeman saying, "Move along, move along." Crankabille wanted to wait to get paid; the policeman took him to jail; while in jail he lost his livelihood. When he got out, it was snowy and cold, and he had no place, no family. He got what he could from the market, the

136

remnants, but nobody would buy them. He saw that he was going to starve and freeze. It was Christmas Eve; he was passing by a great church all lit up pretty, with finely dressed people going in an out. He lingered smelling the good fragrances when a policeman came along and told him to "Move along, move along." Crankabille thought that if he made the policeman mad, he would get arrested and be put back into the warm jail where he would get something to eat. So, he called the policeman a dirty cow, or words to that effect, and the old policeman just looked at him saying, "Move along. It's Christmas, move along." There I was, just as fast as I could write, putting that story to paper.

Do you know, over the years since then, Red Skelton has done a take-off on this old, old French story many times, and made it famous on stage and television.

Later, the head of the Language Department, Mrs. Ludlum, remembered me being in her Latin classes, and she wrote me a lovely note saying what a good showing I had done on the exam. I'm not actually all that proficient in French; I was just lucky.

Who knows? If you like words and you have a fairly retentive memory... I can remember stories and plots and the people in them, but I can't tell you who's related to who right here in this community. Lucille could name everybody and everything about them. Daddy was the same way, but I couldn't. Stories were more real to me. I was very comfortable in that world.

But sometimes it's embarrassing. Just this morning in Church at Salem Fork, Ray Martin, my first cousin, sat behind me and leaned over and said, "Wasn't it terrible about Pete Sneed dying?"

"Pete!" I said. "You mean, our Pete Sneed from just

down the road? Our Pete Sneed from Burch? Why, he's not old enough to die. His old mother up at Guardian Care is ninety-three years old, and she out-lived him?"

Yes, just sixty-four years old. He was buried this afternoon up here at Little Richmond. That's how I am about real people. Some, I can remember, but mostly it's ummm, errr. And when people want me to do recall, it gets to be a problem for me.

Well, I made it through Berea College on my second attempt and graduated with a BA in General Music, and

then went to work. I could have qualified for either voice or instrumental, and what teaching I've done has been in both, along with lots of regular classroom teaching, fourth grade and such. In Kentucky, I had a Provisional High School Certificate, I believe it was called, but I never taught on it. In North Carolina, I had a class "A" Certificate in General Music.

Doris Anthea Martin Gabbard
Graduation Day
Berea College, 1953

Class room teaching involved programs for every holiday of the year. So, there wasn't much of a family spirit at holidays at home because I was always at practice for, or playing, one function or another.

So, that's how it went until I retired, with one break. In 1964 when Mama had her first heart attack, I dropped outside work - all that driving, all those night programs - and did my family duty first.

When I moved home with my children, Taylor stayed with his family. Neither of us sought a divorce, but

A Mother's Day fulfilled back home in Little Richmond, 1954. That's me with Nicholas in arms. To my right is Charlene with Johnny hiding. Alex on my left joins in the fun, whatever it was at the moment. Michaela took the picture.

we certainly didn't have a marriage. Times were quickly becoming tough for his family, and he was the only earner of importance. When he died in 1963, I had been in North Carolina for twelve years, and all of my children called it home. All except Michaela who married and stayed in Kentucky.

139

The
Manhattan Club

Taylor and I met at the Manhattan Club located on
what was then the main road from Berea to
Richmond. The girl in my dormitory who was also a
music major took me with her sometimes when she went
out. Girls didn't like to go out alone, so I wound up tagging
along with her from time to time. She was dating a Berea
boy, and even though we were not supposed to be off
campus or in a car, that's what happened. It was toward the
end of my second year at Berea when we stopped at the
Manhattan Club, and they wanted to dance. Of course, I
was the odd extra.

The Manhattan Club, 1938. Our first home was the two-room bungalow to the left. The "Club" was open 24-hours.

Dancing was to a back room juke box in the space between the booths that lined the walls, and I happened to sit down in the corner booth that allowed me to see into the kitchen. It was located in the left corner of the building, left of the front door. When people came in, they could sit at tables to the right in the front part where a counter with stools was located, or go between the counter and the kitchen to the back room where booths and the juke box were located. Just a few people were there when we came in. I looked back at the couple dancing, knowing that they didn't want me watching them, and I could see a big, fat boy washing dishes in the kitchen, sweating to beat the band. So, I stepped over and asked him if I could come in the kitchen and help him wash dishes.

He looked at me with surprise and said, "Well, yeah." I helped him with the dishes; we chatted, and by the

142

time we left, we had exchanged names. I believe I saw him once again after that, again just a happenstance kind of thing in stopping at the Manhattan Club. It wasn't much of a club, really, just a place to get a sandwich and a cold drink. Mostly truckers stopped off to rest and eat on their way somewhere. The juke box was about the only thing that was "club" about it.

Well, during the following summer, Taylor drove down here to see me, all the way from Kentucky. That was some trip in those days. He stayed around a couple of days the first time, then went back. We exchanged letters a time or two, and the second time he came down, why, I made the fateful decision.

As the old folks said, I jumped the broom. We got married in July. I don't know why, really. I've often wondered why I did that; I was in college doing very well, heading for something I thought I wanted to do, but I must not have been so sure about that, either. I suppose it has something to do with.... People look more attractive if you don't know much about them. Biology does the rest, that's about the only answer.

If you are simpatico with someone, it's the old thing about the grass being greener on the other side. Let's face it, if you're under your parent's thumb, and you're told what to do at every turn, it's attractive to think that you might be allowed your freedom by slipping out into marriage. Little do you know that with that freedom you're going to wind yourself up into all kinds of knots, but it takes years to discover that.

We hit if off very well, right from the beginning; conversation mostly. I didn't meet his family until after we were married. I was a country girl with long hair that I

143

braided and coiled around my head. Maybe he liked a country-fied girl.... I don't know what he liked about me, but we had some pretty nice children together. Taylor was eight years older than me, a big, generous fellow, just as pleasant and kind as he could be. Nobody said a bad word about him. Anything in the world he had was mine as well. The fact that he ended up with nothing, that was mine, too.

We were married during the summer of 1937, July, in Dobson at the Methodist Parsonage. Hazel Sprinkle and the Register of Deeds, Bertha Shinault, went with us as witnesses. We left that evening and drove up through North Wilkesboro, up through West Virginia and on into Akron, Ohio. We overnighted at a place where the truck drivers were well known. We stayed there a couple of nights, then went on down to Berea. The residence behind the Manhattan Club was our first home. The club was located on the right side of the Route 25E on the way to Richmond.

Carl Myracle was the co-owner of the Manhattan Club. There really wasn't much income from it, not for two young families, and Carl - maybe it was his wife - decided to sell out his share to Taylor. What looked like a pretty good thing for us turned out to die on the vine. In the second year, 1938, a new road to Richmond was built and it by-passed the Manhattan Club, the traffic went away, and our business collapsed.

During that time, we lived in the little 2-room house out back of the Manhattan Club. It was either that or the Dr.'s house down on Elder Street, and for a time during the war we rented the house located kind of diagonally across from the Dr.'s house. Then, when we got enough money ahead, we bought the house and property on High Street, but it wasn't too many years later that we lost that house.

144

I made curtains for our 2-roomer; his Grandmother Rachel gave us an old couch; his mother, Bell, had already given him a stout iron bed: he was such a heavy man that a wooden bed would not hold him up. Taylor was about three hundred pounds. His top weight, about ten years later, was about three sixty-five. By then, I had been making his clothes for years; it was hard to find a fifty-four inch waist trouser. I learned to make his clothes at the same time that I learned to make children's clothes.

The Manhattan Club wasn't really a club, it was just a beer joint, a roadhouse in today's parlance, where people could get a meal or a sandwich and a cold drink. Big long Blue Flash coolers lined the area behind the bar, and at least ten lines of bottled beer were offered to customers who stated their preferences. We made a plate lunch for the truck drivers, whatever kind of meat we had on hand, vegetables and bread. Beef stew maybe. Once in a while I'd make up a big batch of meatballs and tomato sauce so that we could serve spaghetti quickly. In the summertime we tried to keep homemade potato salad in the refrigerator, very plain kinds of things like that. We didn't have a menu, everything was a "blue plate special," just the food we had on hand, or sandwiches we could make. If someone wanted bacon and eggs, we could prepare it for them, or maybe pork chops with eggs on the side, a little ham, maybe, but mostly it was what we were eating, just more of it. The lights were on and someone was at the counter twenty-four hours of the day, every day. Twelve on, twelve off got very boring.

There was no conversation, and if you didn't have anything to read, about all there was to do was put slugs in the juke box and listen to every record until you knew every pause, every word. We had absolutely no social life. We never went to church, and the way they did things was the way it was.

Once in a while a customer would stagger in all red-eyed and ask, "How about some milk toast?" Well, we'd make it if we could, whatever they might ask for. The truck drivers were comfortable there.

Squinting into the sun with Margaret and the "Fresh Gardner," 1939. The Manhattan Club wasn't far from going under.

The first time I prepared milk toast, I thought I'd done the job perfectly. The way my mother did it was to spread butter lightly on two slices of bread and put them in the oven to brown on both sides, then put them in a soup bowl and pour hot milk over them. The toast would drink the milk. That's how she made it for her mother, my "little" granny Flora, who lived with us off and on for several years after being forced out of her home in East Bend.

Taylor's sister, Margaret, took one look at it and

said, "Oh my goodness. Throw that out." And she did. She went in the kitchen and browned two pieces of bread, cut them into little squares, put them in a pan, poured in cold milk and brought it to a boil. That sort of thing gave me little reason to be comfortable.

We spent our first winter there in the residence behind the club, two small rooms. We had a family pretty fast. Michaela was born the next spring, 1938, in May. All during Michaela's first baby-hood years, we had gypsies who came and asked to camp in one corner of the lot. There was a large field off to the right of the lot in back where they took up residence; they had a bunch of vans and tents. The field accommodated all of them, several families, and they paid us a little something for the use of the land. They were rather entertaining, and they enjoyed my baby, and I enjoyed their baby though learning a lot about the differences in childcare.

With Michaela, summer 1938

They never had a diaper on their child; a carpet was spread on the ground where the child was attended to, but I never saw a wet spot or anything dirty about the carpet. They picked the child up occasionally and tended to nature without having to bother with the diaper thing. The ladies

147

were good mothers, and the men worked all around there doing all the jobs that gypsy men do. I didn't talk with them much; women didn't, you know.

The gypsies had all kinds of vehicles. There were one or two cars with trailers pulled behind. Those were the families that had the tents. One or two had an early form of van, sort of like what we called delivery trucks, nothing fancy. They led a quiet existence; I didn't notice any big hoopdedoos. Their family lives seemed to be more or less like everyone else's.

One of the ladies was on up in her eighties and her hair was still coal black. It was so long that she could sit on it, and every morning she would sit out in the sun and brush and brush her hair before she put it up. I seem to recall that she used oil of some sort. I complimented on what beautiful hair she had, and the only thing she said was, "White women wash their hair too much."

When the weather began getting cold, it was suggested that with undependable heat, it would be best for the baby if we moved into the Dr.'s house. So, we did. There wasn't much time for togetherness because Taylor was working the business, and I was with his family. I never became completely comfortable with the situation, and when they closed the old Route 25E to truck traffic when the new road was completed, things got quieter and quieter. Taylor closed the Manhattan Club and went to work driving for Roadway Express based out of Akron.

Then I was doubly dissatisfied; no place to call home and a guest with a baby in someone else's home. The day came that a cousin, Clyde Marshall, was driving a truck headed for Akron, and I spoke to him saying that I would like to pack a bag and go along with him. If I couldn't find a place to live there, then I'd just go on back home to North Carolina. He was taking a chance, because his insurance could have been canceled. At one point along the way, at a check point, I crouched down out of sight and put a blanket over me. Clyde eased on through, and we went on to Akron.

Taylor and I took for us one of those tiny two-room, second floor apartments over a store in South Akron. Over across the street, another of the truck drivers, Ben Parks, had taken a whole upstairs over a store and furnished all the bedrooms with nothing but beds. He had them turned every which way so that there was just navigating space between them. Even the screened-in back porch had beds in it; cold in the winter. He had a large living room and a big kitchen with a long table in it. It was an overnight sleep-and-eat establishment just for truck drivers; sometimes more than one night. He kept some girls in to do the cooking and serving and cleaning. They set the table country style.

Once in a while just before Johnny was born, Ben got caught without the girls to help him. They couldn't make it for some reason, such as Monday mornings after a big weekend, and he ran over and got me. He'd say, "Come and oversee the kitchen. We'll peel the potatoes, and do everything. You just put it all together." So, I didn't do much work; my job was to see to it that everything was on the table at the same time.

By that time it was early spring, and I was getting pretty heavy on my feet. Some of them asked, "When are you expecting that baby?"

"It won't be too much longer now, that's for sure," I said.

Well, all those truck drivers were very nice to me

149

and threw a baby shower for me. They all got together and someone went to a store and bought a complete layette for me. That was in the spring of 1940 just before Johnny was born. Taylor was transferred to the Atlanta run about then, and they knew that we were leaving Akron, so they invited me over one day and showered me.

Meanwhile, Michaela went right along with me. She was a two year old toddler, and those truck drivers would tell her stories, play with her, and keep her occupied while I was on kitchen duty. It was a very neighborly kind of arrangement that went on for the better part of a year, although my involvement in the kitchen was just a few times.

At that stage, a toddler can be a handful, and Michaela was. When I heard a mighty crash from the kitchen, I ran - or waddled - to see what could possibly have happened. Michaela had climbed up our open face breakfront and pulled it over on herself, breaking virtually every dish and glass in the process, but doing nothing more than scaring herself silly. I think she still has an intact bowl from that episode.

With Johnny's arrival growing nearer by the day and Taylor newly assigned to Roadway's Atlanta terminal, I followed him from Akron and hunted around and found an apartment nearby for us, paid the rent and moved in. The place required an all-day cleaning, and when bed time came, I was quite naturally exhausted. Michaela was in a crib by the bed, and along about midnight restless noises aroused me. I turned on the light and discovered my child literally covered with bedbugs - they were coming out of the walls everywhere. Well, I hoisted her out, cleaned her up and we went to the nearest hotel for the rest of the night.

In following Taylor with Michaela a toddler and Johnny just a short time away, I realized that without living quarters ready to move into, I couldn't go it. The next day I packed everything up and drove back home to my father's farm where Johnny was born shortly afterwards. It seemed that everything pulled in all sorts of directions except those that brought our family together.

Taylor Price Gabbard, 1939

The Dr.'s house was solid, and though not a fine place, it was of a good size with all the conveniences. The front yard bordering Elder Street had a sidewalk leading to a broad porch and the front door. Two large trees provided shade, and the Dr. was in the habit of parking his big black car under them. From the porch, the front door led into a double room with an arched divider in the middle. Off to the left was a bedroom with a closet in the left corner. Beyond it on the opposite wall was a large walk-in closet, and through it was the corner bedroom. That was Margaret's room. Her bed sat in the far corner; that was where she

151

died. Adjoining this room was another bedroom that led to the bathroom. From this bedroom was the large dining room that made the circuit to the double front room. Off to the right of the last bedroom I mentioned was the door to the basement, a full basement that gave the house a lot of room. Sort of built on as an extra was the kitchen with a step down from the dining room, and from it was a screened-in back porch along the wall adjoining the dining room. The porch had steps down to the back yard and the pawpaw trees, then the garden and barn further on.

The last time I saw the back porch, there was the Dr.'s dental chair and all kinds of stuff from his profession packed in along with things from Taylor's house, none of it worth much of anything. And it wasn't long before that house, too, was lost. Seems like that family just couldn't keep things together.

While visiting, Taylor and I stayed in the front bedroom by the front porch, but we had taken up living arrangements in our little house at the Manhattan Club. I made it as homey as I could, but we didn't spend much time there, or anywhere, really; we were working all the time. We worked twelve on and twelve off, and tried to cover as much of the eating trade as we could. Our menus were mostly what we cooked for ourselves in much larger quantities, along with sandwiches that could be prepared quickly, cold drinks, packaged food things like crackers and potato chips, that sort thing.

Before becoming a dentist, James Chester Gabbard was a carpenter. He and his father, William H. "Uncle Mike" Gabbard, came down from Owsley County to work for Berea College at the time that the college hospital was being built, among other new buildings, and they were all well

152

constructed, too. One of the nurses told me that Uncle Mike hung every door in Berea College hospital.

Chester decided that he wanted to study dentistry. So, he went to Louisville, and his wife, Bell, went to work cooking for a hotel located in the west end of Berea. She cooked, and he went to school until he came out with his DDS and came back to Berea. He set up his practice above the drug store just up the street from Boone Tavern, and they soon negotiated to buy a house on down Prospect Street from his Daddy's house. Up until then they had been living in the same house with his parents, Uncle Mike's house, on the corner of Prospect and Elder, but it wasn't long until Chester and Bell lost their new house. Rachel, Uncle Mike's wife, told me one day that there wasn't enough income from dentistry to pay for the house.

So, they were back with Uncle Mike and Rachel. Behind their house was a large garden spot for a plot or two, then a one-story frame house further on. It wasn't nearly as nice a house as they had tried to make a home, but that was where Chester and Bell ended up. It faced westerly on Elder while Uncle Mike's house faced southward on Prospect. Behind their new home was another garden, then a barn where they kept a cow in the wintertime. In the summertime they pastured the cow where there was grass.

Later a street was cut through quite close to the house, but back then, all that area from the barn to the creek was a quite large, open field. Bell often gathered up wild creasy greens around the edges of the field and along the creek bank. All that area became a housing development in the 1950s.

The Gabbards had come from Indian Creek in Owsley County, and Dr. Gabbard told tales about hearing the women at their Monday morning wash with their "battling" boards beating the clothes down at the creek. Apparently, there wasn't much in Owsley County, even roads, back then. Bell told me that if she went anywhere, she went by horseback, and with two young children, she put Margaret behind her and Taylor in front of her where she handled both him and the reins. Their third child, Junior, was born after they came from Owsley County to Berea.

Margaret was a big woman, like Taylor was a big man, but Junior was a trim, fine looking young man when I married Taylor. He was a year or two or three younger, and he worked around the Manhattan Club for a while. Then he did some truck driving. When he married a young woman from London on down Route 25 below Berea, the next thing you know, Junior and his new wife had latched onto a cottage rental/stopover place just out of the city. They ran their business for several years, then moved on to Florida.

Dr. Gabbard was a fine singer. He belonged to the Harmonia Society. They presented "The Messiah" at Christmas and another performance at Easter, as I recall. He loved to sing. He was also prominent in the Masonic Lodge. I think he was High Priest of the Kentucky Lodge, a Knight Templar and had a wonderful uniform, complete with sword and shako worn for ceremonies. At his untimely death, not yet an old man, he was buried with Mason's full honors. He was just 61; he got out of bed one Sunday morning and fell dead.

There were a couple of older men, also Lodge fellows, who came in a night a week and played Setback. I'd never learned to play cards, so I had to be taught. Taylor was a great card player, also a Mason, but I never enjoyed cards all that much. After a while I could sort of hold my own occasionally, but card playing held little interest for me.

Dr. Gabbard and Taylor belonged to the Masonic Lodge York Rite. Playing cards at the Masonic Lodge was a favorite way for them to pass the time. I don't recall that they went to the lodge in Richmond to play cards, but they did attend certain meetings there.

Like all Masonic Lodges, the one in Richmond was upstairs. Sometime in the late 1940s there was a fire at the Richmond lodge, and among the things that were damaged by smoke were an antique pump organ and a square grand piano. Taylor bought both for $50 and brought them home.

Our house on High Street was built so that you could look from the front door, through a door into the hall, and straight to the bathroom. The living room was immediately on the left as you came into the house, and there was a fireplace with built-in bookcases on the outside wall. The downstairs bedroom door opened to the left off the hall before reaching the bathroom, and the kitchen door opened to the right at the end of the hall. Just to the right as you went into the kitchen was the door that led to the basement. To the right of the front door there was an archway that led to the flight of stairs to the second level. They rose up against the left wall of the dining room. It was possible to go around and around the house, and Michaela did just that ad nauseum the winter she got roller skates. Those hardwood floors and skates with hard metal wheels; I earned a star in my crown for letting her learn to skate on them!

155

The upstairs consisted of two bedrooms, one in front divided by a door to the larger room in the back. The latter included a walk-in closet and attic space. There was an oil furnace for heat, but the ductwork didn't extend to the upstairs bedrooms that got whatever warmth they did from the open stairway and a grate fitted into the floor directly above the one into the living room. The children could peep through that grate and spy on the goings-on downstairs after they had been banished to bed.

The square grand was made of rosewood, and it was a thing of beauty after it was cleaned. The four legs were intricately carved; its finish was gorgeous. At first it was placed against the wall just inside the front door, so the door to the hall always stood ajar because the piano took up the entire wall. Later it was moved to a spot in front of the living room windows, and one Christmas all of the children very nearly caught Santa Claus going up the chimney when a train whistle attracted them. There was Johnny's new Lionel train set up under the square grand piano. Needless to say, there was no more sleeping that Christmas Eve! He still has the train; one of our family's better moments treasured every since.

The little organ needed a new bellows, among other things, before it could be played, so I set to the chore. It had been manufactured by the Estey Organ Company in Brattleboro, Vermont, and I was pleasantly surprised to learn that they were still in business. I wrote to them and asked about getting a new bellows. In due time, the new bellows arrived and was installed. What sweet music that little pump organ made! I played it and sang to its melodies for hours and could not have predicted that was to influence children for many years to come.

The square grand piano had no foot pedals, so it wasn't easy to control the echo. Although a fine instrument, it didn't provide as much pleasure as the pump organ. When I was working on my big project for my music classes at Berea College, I had to transcribe a piece of music for a complete orchestra, and I played that little organ almost nonstop for days on end.

I wanted to give each of my children the gift of music, and Michaela, being first, became rather accomplished on the clarinet. She played her clarinet as I accompanied her at the organ keyboard, and I like to think that we made beautiful music.

Once when a boyfriend came to escort her to a basketball game at Berea High School - it wasn't really a date because she was only 14 or 15 at the time - she was tootling away with me on the organ, and when we finished there was her beau standing at the front door, listening and watching. She was terribly embarrassed, but I think he was favorably impressed.

Later, when I returned to North Carolina to teach, the only piece of furniture other than bedsteads and a few other absolutely essential things that I brought was that little pump organ. Ben drove to Berea in Daddy's Chevrolet pickup and hauled everything back home for me. I drove my car down with my four younger children.

That organ enriched the lives of many students at the Little Richmond School for years, though it was damaged by vandalous boys one time. It now resides in Michaela's house, one of her proudest possessions. It still plays - but with a squeak. During 1982, she had it refinished and had another new bellows installed. The Estey Organ Company provided it.

That little organ dates back to at least the early 1800s, so it's a real treasure. What amazes me is that the Estey Organ Company is still in business. That's longevity!

When Taylor went to driving for Roadway Express, he was on the Akron, Ohio to Gadsden, Alabama run, and his route was along Route 25 through Berea. So, he was in and out as he went through. After a while I realized that this was going to be a permanent thing, so I went to Akron with him. Then it was to Atlanta when he was transferred to that run, then back here to the farm in North Carolina where Johnny was born, then to Charlotte where Charlene was born, then the war came along, and we went back to Berea when Taylor got a job at the Blue Grass Ordinance Depot. Alex and Nicholas were my Berea babies. Truck drivers moved a lot, and I went with him.

The Dr. and Mrs. Gabbard, we called them Paw and Maw, had three children, Margaret, Taylor and James Chester, Jr. Margaret married a Berea College student from West Virginia, a Robert Wilmont Nichols, and they had a child, a boy with the same given name. We called him Bobby. During this time, when he was just a little boy maybe four or five, he got badly burned.

His uncle had given him a little pipe, and Bobby went around pretending to smoke his pipe. He also carried around an old lantern, along with a box of matches, and played at lighting them. There was an old car parked on the gravel road that ran beside the house and on down by the barn into the field bordered on the opposite end by a large creek. One day Taylor was asleep in the side bedroom right beside the car, he had been working nights, and was in the midst of a sound snooze when there was a sudden, tremendous, WHOOMP! That old car still had gasoline in the tank, nobody paid much attention to it, and Bobby had screwed off the lid and struck a match to see down into it. His face....

They rushed that child to the hospital and stayed right with him night and day. Poor little Bobby was terribly burned. Through it all the doctors and his family did a masterful job with his recovery. As he grew, he didn't have a single scar that I recall. It was miraculous.

Mr. Nichols' connection to, and departure from, the Gabbard family occurred while he was attending Berea College. I don't know how he got acquainted with Margaret, but the day came when he was at Dr. Gabbard's house with his new wife, who was expecting. The boys, Taylor and Junior, had an air rifle that they were shooting out back of the house near suppertime. He went out with them, only to have Margaret recall him sternly, "Wilmont! You get right back into this house."

Well, apparently he did just that, in the back door, through the house, and out the front door. When it came supper time, Mr. Nichols couldn't be found. I don't know that he ever saw his son, Bobby. So far as I know, he was never heard from again.

In time there was a second husband for Margaret, a Mr. Charles MacDonald, called "Mac." He and Margaret married, and they soon had a child, a girl this time. She was named JoAnn. He was around there just a little because they lived in Cincinnati where he worked. So, they spent most of their time up there. I don't remember where JoAnn was born, but Margaret was soon back home with her baby; Mr. MacDonald had died. Both Bobby and JoAnn grew up in the Dr.'s house just as if they were his children, not grand-children.

Margaret died of Hodgkin's disease (leukemia) in the early 1950s, leaving both her children in her parent's care, and then Dr. Gabbard died, too; all very sorrowful and unexpected. About then, the youngest son, Junior, married and moved away. So, there was Mrs. Gabbard, Bell, with two young children and only Taylor, her eldest son earning anything. He and I were separated by then, and he was providing nothing for his own children; just trying to keep the homeplace together, but things went steadily down hill.

Their only source of income was from the "Stand," a soft ice cream business. Its menu of soft ice cream, sand-wiches and such was popular for a time, but without upkeep to make the place inviting for drive-by customers, business tapered off.

Behind the "Stand" was a large open field that had been in tobacco prior to the Dr.'s purchase, and it suited the carnivals that came to Berea every year. Managed right, that could have been a money maker, but in the end, little money was made, and Taylor faced enormous clean-up jobs that cost still more money.

Well, I stayed with it for six children. One between Johnny and Charlene didn't make it. Nicholas was my last, five that survived and thrived.

After Taylor died a relatively young man at 51, in 1964, it was about a year later that Jacob Michael and I were married. He was a long time friend of ours from the truck driving days.

Rachel

&

"Uncle Mike"

During the two years that Michaela was a boarding student at Foundation, she would sneak off from time to time and go visit her grandparents, Paw and Maw Gabbard, as the children called them. It's the job of the first grandchild to name the grandparents, and she provided the handles that stuck. All the grandchildren since then called the Gabbard elders Paw and Maw.

It was during her visits that she learned about the

Gabbard family, and subsequently passed on what I know about that side of the family.

Their hard scrabble lives in the backwoods mountains of Kentucky produced a lot of entertaining stories, but I've forgotten most of them. One that stands out was Bell's telling about Taylor's birth.

They were still living in Owsley County when her time came, and Chester went for the midwife. Margaret, their first born, was about two years old and was asleep in the bed beside Bell.

Bell described her labors as never being very long, and it quickly became obvious that the new baby was going to be born before Chester could get back, so she just lay there and muffled her groans to keep from waking Margaret. She delivered Taylor by herself. When Chester and the midwife arrived, the new baby was lying between her legs as he had been born. He was a big baby - eleven pounds, I think she said - so she must have suffered terribly, but her concern for Margaret was such that she wouldn't do anything to wake her up and get her upset.

James Chester, Jr., always called Junior, was born after the Gabbards moved to Berea. When his time came near, Chester wasn't around again, and Bell walked from their house along the edge of the large garden between the two houses to "Uncle Mike" and Rachel's house to get help.

She described "Uncle Mike" as saying that as soon as her foot hit the porch he knew what was going on and put his pants on while on the run to the door. Bell made it back home, and the doctor arrived in time to deliver Junior, so she didn't have to make that delivery alone.

Rachel and "Uncle Mike" were an unlikely pair; he was a likeable kind of man, she was quite the opposite. My recollections of them are not very complete because I wasn't around all that much. "Uncle Mike" died when Michaela was little, so she has few recollections of them as well.

Rachel was stingy - there's no other word for it, really. She'd bake a pie or cake and rather than share it with "Uncle Mike," she'd hide it on top of a cabinet and eat it when he was out of the house. In those days milk wasn't homogenized, so there was a thick layer of cream at the top of the bottle. Rachel would carefully pour off this cream and use it in her coffee or whatever, and poor "Uncle Mike" had to use skim milk.

After "Uncle Mike" died, Rachel lived with Chester and Bell for a while, and her house stood empty for several years, until the early 1950s, I think. The Doctor's house was comfortable, well constructed, but it had the odd add-on of a kitchen and back porch. From the substantial dining room, a door led into the kitchen by way of a step down with the appliances to the left. To the right was the door leading to the screened-in back door. The kitchen table was built in against the far wall to the left, under the windows. Above the seat on the right was where Bell kept her violets in colorful little planters in a rack on the wall. The table ana benches were made like a booth in a restaurant. One day while they were eating lunch, Rachel looked up at Paw and said, "Chester, I have the most awful pain in my chest," and then she just pitched forward and died right there on the table.

The James Chester Gabbard family c. 1931. (l to r) Junior, Margaret, Chester, Taylor and Bell in a "formal" photo in their Berea home.

The dining room was dominated by a large table in the center, a full size buffet by the wall opposite the windows that looked out over the back porch. A refrigerator sat at the left wall near the door to the kitchen. To the right of the dining room was the long family room with its wide arch way from the dining room. In the left corner by the arch was a fine glass front display containing Chester's mustache cups, fine china, and other prized items that Bell had collected. Rather than for meals, this table was used most often for card playing.

The kitchen booth was where the family assembled for meals. This table was the scene of many an argument, I'm sure, because the Gabbards were quarrelsome folks. Once when Taylor, Margaret and Junior were still young, an

165

argument erupted over something during supper. Taylor provided some insult or other, and Margaret threw her fork at him. It stuck in his cheek just to the right of his mouth. I suppose it wasn't a bad wound, but if she'd hit a little higher the fork would have gone into his eye.

Like Taylor, Margaret had a quick temper, and she was bossy. I wonder if she ever regretted any of her nastiness in later years when she was so sick. The last summer before Margaret died, Michaela walked from the house on High Street across town two or three times a week to visit with her and play cards. By then she could get around the house only by holding onto a straight back chair that she pushed in front of her. It was a sad time, and I like to think that Michaela brought a little sunshine into an otherwise dismal existence.

"Uncle Mike," Rachel, Margaret, Chester; they went in quick succession, it seems. There just didn't seem to be any good luck in that family.

In the evenings "Uncle Mike" would walk up the path from his house to the Dr.'s to listen to the Philco radio. He must have been as deaf as a post, because he'd turn the volume up as high as he could and then cup his ear to listen to the news.

That tall radio of fine wood cabinetry sat in the main room of the Dr.'s house from their time through my children's, and it always worked, but it was more of a fascinating relic to them after the coming of television. It sat by the window with a comfortable, overstuffed chair between it and the fireplace on the back wall opposite the front door.

An upright piano sat in various locations in the room, but mostly by the door to the middle bedroom and adjacent to the arch that divided the main room at its center. The piano was rarely, if ever, played and was finally moved into the middle bedroom to block passage through the large walk-in closet leading to the corner bedroom.

While Margaret lay dying, the children were kept out of her room, and Michaela got into trouble for making noise plinking on the way-out-of-tune piano to amuse herself.

"Uncle Mike," Rachel, Chester and Bell grew up in the horse and buggy era when the pace of life was considerably slower. Chester was the first to drive reasonably well, considering that there were no tests for drivers when the first automobiles were being sold to the general public. I don't know when he got his first car, but I do know that he came within a hair's breadth of buying the farm several times while driving it.

Michaela recalls that riding with Chester was an adventure for the children and a heart-stopping experience for any adults who happened to be in the car. Every year or so, Chester went back to Owsley County to visit relatives, and the car would be going from one shoulder to the other as he craned to point out familiar landmarks. Amazingly, he

167

Isabell Combs Gabbard c. 1925 and Dr. James Chester Gabbard c. 1940, Taylor's parents, both born in Owsley County, Kentucky

never had an accident on any of those trips.

His car was always parked under a tree in front of the house, there being no garage. He was an impatient person and hated to be kept waiting, especially when he was waiting in the car. Many times when he and Bell would be going somewhere he'd get in the car and, when she didn't come out immediately, he'd start blowing the horn. Poor Bell! She was so embarrassed because all the neighbors heard the commotion, but she'd just get more angry with him. Michaela recalls seeing her face, red as a beet, and she's often wondered what, if anything, Bell said to Chester when they were alone in the car.

His dental office was on the short street that in-cluded Boone Tavern, and he customarily parked his car as close to the entrance to the stairs as he could. When he came downstairs to drive home, he always walked out to the street behind the car, looked carefully up and down the street, and, satisfied that the way was clear, got in the car, started it up, and backed out without looking again. There were dozens of near misses, thanks to the vigilance of other drivers, but he did back into at least one car. I don't remember the outcome of that fender bender other than that nobody was hurt, but Chester was outraged. After all, he HAD checked to be sure there was nobody behind the car before he backed out!

The city cemetery was on the outskirts of town on the old road to Richmond, and from time to time Chester would stop by to visit the folks who had gone before. There was a wide driveway that turned off the road and then made a left turn into the cemetery through iron gates set in the stone fence.

The road through the cemetery made a loop to accommodate driving around without having to retrace your path. Chester's last car was a big green Packard, and he loved it. One nice day he had been to the cemetery and, upon leaving, he went through his normal ritual of stopping the car inside the gates, walking to the road, looking up and down, then getting back into the car and pulling out into the road. This time he pulled out in front of a car that was barreling along, not expecting an old man to suddenly appear in the road in front of him, and that was the end of the Packard. Fortunately, Paw wasn't hurt other than being shaken up and sore, but I think the other driver was hurt a little. Both cars were total wrecks. There were some whispers about possible lawsuits, but I think he offered up enough money to buy the other driver another car and that was that.

The dental practice probably would have supported the family handsomely, except that Chester kept no books other than in his head. Unfortunately, the folks who owed him weren't willing to 'fess up and pay up when he died, so Bell got nothing. There's no telling how many people in Berea still have fillings that Dr. Gabbard put in for them and that they never paid for.

Chester was an excellent carpenter - a cabinet maker, I think is the term - and he did some beautiful work with wood. He also had some skill carving. Unbeknownst to the family, he carved a mold for a cameo-style ring and he used the gold for fillings mixed with copper or brass to cast rings for the ladies of the family. Bell got the first one, then Margaret, then me. Michaela got the last one. There's no telling what happened to Bell's and Margaret's rings, but mine was handed down to Charlene. Somehow, she lost it. Michaela still has hers, but the gold is so soft and wears away so easily that she won't wear it. Someday, I suspect that she will hand it down to one of the family members as a treasured heirloom.

Rachel and "Uncle Mike," along with Bell and

Chester, exist only in my memories, though prodded along by Michaela's recollections. And my children who remember them. Their branch of the Gabbard family tree didn't produce many others who might be interested. They were fine folks, I'm sure, eccentric in their ways as we all are, but that just adds colorful facets to their lives that would, otherwise, be mostly forgotten.

Family Times

With Michaela, Johnny and Charlene, summer of '44

The period of time that we lived in Charlotte was when Michaela was 4 or 5 and Johnny was a toddler. If his favorite thing to do wasn't taking his clothes off and wandering around the house, inside or out, it was spooning up dirt and eating it. Two little imps were a handful, and seeing a giggly little boy running around buck naked was a source of amusement at times, but dirt - that really bothered me. I just couldn't accept that.

We were living on Merriman Avenue not far from

172

the Roadway terminal, and one day Michaela came screaming home holding her chin and seeming to bleed from
everywhere. It scared me half to death, but I was relieved to
discover that it was just a flesh wound; she had sneaked off
to visit a little girl friend and fallen up the brick steps of
their house hitting her chin on the edge of a step.

Little Michaela got
her first real spanking in
that house when she
decided that it was time
for a fire in the living
room fireplace. She had
struck nearly an entire
box of matches trying
to light the log. Taylor
really warmed her behind;
fires were scary things
and known to roar
through those wood
frame houses in a hurry.

Michaela at ten

We were living in
a rental house, one of those
little frame structures with
small rooms, a little front
porch and a fireplace. Most of them were about the same
size and catered to young families. We moved next door
when the third child came along; we needed more room.

That was a difficult time; the next one after Johnny
didn't make it, stillborn at 8 months. It just broke my heart
every time I looked at the layette I had made for the baby,
and I broke down and cried. Time took care of things,
though, and I packed up everything and took it to the

Johnny at ten

Florence Crittendon Home for unwed mothers. It was put to good use, I'm sure.

Of course, most of the mothers put their babies up for adoption and held their secret to their dying day because it was a scandal of the first order to have a baby out of wedlock in those days. Somehow, I think that would be worse than losing a baby.

Jacob Michael and H. B. Wolfe, friends and fellow Roadway drivers with Taylor, were frequent visitors to our Merriman Avenue house. We all became good friends, lifelong friends. Taylor was assigned a long haul route to Atlanta, and Jacob would meet him in a pre-arranged location to swap trucks so that Taylor could be at home every night with his family. Jacob was a bachelor and didn't mind staying overnight in Atlanta. H. B. and Jacob always brought presents to the children when they came to visit. Later, H. B. took a fancy to Lucille and ended up my brother-in-law. Much later, Jacob became my second husband after Taylor's passing.

In time, another new baby came into the Gabbard home. Charlene was born while we lived in Charlotte.

Christmas in the Martin household was never a big production with a decorated tree and all the pagan customs we've incorporated into our celebration of the Christ Child's birth. At most, there was a quick visit from Saint Nick on Christmas Eve as he dropped off a box of presents on the front porch for all the good little girls and boys, then scurried along.

One Christmas, Taylor was to be on the road, so the family did the best we could without him. It was a cold, snowy time that added to the excitement of the season because it was not uncommon for mid-day temperatures to climb into the 70s in late December. The children especially liked the wintry atmosphere. And then, Taylor surprised us all. He had parked his truck in somebody's barnyard and came to have Christmas with us.

The parlor was large but unused, kept closed and unheated in the winter. We gathered around the front room, which was also Mama and Daddy's bedroom, and were warming by the stove when a loud CLUNK was heard on the front porch. Somebody said, "I thought I saw a sleigh go by," and that was all it took.

The children raced outside and found a big cardboard box with treasures inside. Michaela got her first camera, a Kodak Brownie that she put to immediate use, and Alex got a fire truck. Johnny and Charlene also got nice presents, but the camera and the fire truck proved to be the lasting combination. Actually, the new toy truck lasted only long enough for Michaela to get a picture of it. Alex was so proud of his new fire engine that he didn't want to share it with Johnny and stomped it into the ground rather than give it up. It was a thing of beauty and met such an untimely demise. Alex was showing the Gabbard temper.

Charlene at six

Michaela became quite a proficient photographer. She took her camera to school and asked her classmates to pose for her. Those photographs still grace her photo albums. Many of the photographs in this book are hers; how fortunate we are for that little camera in her hands. She took pictures of life around her that are now wonderful memories.

Christmas in Kentucky was an entirely different affair. Bell saw to it that a fine tree marked the occasion. The angel on top just cleared the ceiling, and each year she decorated it in a single color scheme with angel hair, making it a most beautiful thing. The tree sat directly across the living room from the front door, making it the centerpiece for everyone entering the house. She placed blue bulb electric candles in every window, and there were stockings for fruits and nuts. But the children had to wait for Christmas Day to open gifts, not the night before as was the custom in the Martin house.

One Christmas, Bell allowed Michaela to help her with Santa Claus gifts for the "little" children. She was 8 or 9 years old and felt so grown up when she assured Johnny and Charlene that there really was a Santa Claus!

176

In 1941 when the Japanese bombed Pearl Harbor, we were living in Charlotte, NC. Taylor was working for Roadway Express, and the word came from his kinfolks back in Kentucky that an Ordinance Depot for the war effort was being built between Berea and Richmond, and they were taking applications for all kinds of jobs. His family wanted to know if he didn't want to make application, and he did for some aspect of transportation. They accepted him subject to a personal interview. He went to Kentucky in 1942, was interviewed, and was hired on the spot.

He didn't come back to Charlotte. I had to close the house, pack up everything, dispose of the furniture, and join him later. It was cold weather, the winter of 1942-'43. My neighbors in Charlotte conveyed us, my children, Michaela, Johnny, Charlene, and me to the train. There was no question of driving at that time; civilian driving was severely curtailed and the trains were very slow and crowded with soldiers going here and there. We made it through all right, and we rented a house in Berea right across the street, diagonally a little to the south, from the James Chester Gabbard house. Taylor had moved back home.

We lived there during the period when he worked at the Blue Grass Ordinance Depot as Transportation Superintendent. The Depot was a storage facility for all sizes of ordinance and was serviced by all types of military vehicles from great big trucks to little jeeps to carry-alls. It was Taylor's job to train girls as chauffeurs because all the men were off being soldiers. So, he trained quite a few girls, and in his office they took calls for whoever needed to go wherever any time of day. Out would go one of his girl drivers with a military vehicle to take care of the request.

Taylor and his B.G.O.D. girls, 1943

Anybody on the post who needed motor transport would call to the Transportation Center. Sometimes vehicles were provided on a regular basis, like taking somebody's children into Richmond every day to school, or picking them up after school, or taking people to the doctor, meeting trains of arriving and departing personnel; taking soldiers wherever they needed to go. Taylor worked there until well after the war when the Depot was mothballed.

During the war, one of Taylor's girls stayed in the house with us as a boarder. Her name was Minerva Witt. She was a divorcee with two children who lived out in the country, and when she got a job at the Ordinance Depot, we gave her a room in our house in exchange for help with the children so I could get out a little in the evening and go to the library, whatever I needed to do. Later, she married and moved to Louisville, and the last I heard of her was that she was driving a cab. So, her experience driving probably gave her an in to that job.

Taylor was a large man. He was at least six feet-one and so big that we couldn't find clothes to fit him. So, I made his clothes. I used a razor blade and split a pair of his trousers apart, starched the pieces heavily, ironed them to make them stiff so that I had a pattern to cut by. I found that the only really hard thing about making pants was the hip pockets. After a fashion, I became rather proficient at making clothes for him. He wore a jacket I made all during the war years when he was Transportation Superintendent at the Blue Grass Ordinance Depot. I was able to find the Army color of woolen material for it, and I made a little suit for Johnny out of the scraps; two full suits of Mother-made clothes. I still have a picture of little Johnny in his suit. It's a treasure of mine. He's also on the cover of this book in it.

Taylor wore a size 13 shoe, and he had a 54-inch waist line. His weight was over three hundred pounds. That's why it was a little hard to see why a person with his problems, diabetic and such, would get into the restaurant business as he did later on. It's hard not to sit around and munch with tasty morsels within reach.

All the employees of the Ordinance Depot, including Taylor, drove their own vehicles from home to the depot each day, parked their cars, and took their assigned military vehicle on to their jobs. For him, it was just like a cab company. The phone would ring and Major whoever would need a four-capacity, a ten-capacity, or whatever kind of vehicle, at a certain time and place. The depot was so large, acres and acres, that no one walked from one point to another. They ordered up a vehicle, and Taylor and his BGOD girls took care of the need.

We had taken our savings, a goodly little bundle because he was paid well during this period, and bought the house on High Street in Berea. After the war, there was a time when he had a little money to work with, and he bought the Studebaker agency in Richmond and commuted each day back and forth. One thing or another happened, and that opportunity went sour rather quickly.

One head shaking thing was that they ruined the motor in a customer's car. The owner, a lady, had left her car for an oil change, and when she picked it up on her way home, she got as far as Paint Lick and the motor seized up. It was dry of oil. They had drained it and had not refilled it. A few things like that, and Taylor didn't have a business.

The agency was located on a corner with the street at the side going up hill to the next traffic light. In that block down from the agency a fire erupted one night, and a paint store went up like a rocket. All those cans of paint exploding and burning; I don't recall the extent of damage, more than one place burned, but the agency survived OK. Of course there was some interruption of customers while the mess was cleared away before business got back to normal. That sort of thing contributed to Taylor's failure as an automobile dealer. Just bad luck, I suppose.

My children. I suspect that every parent goes through the same sort of child rearing woes, but when those woes are your own, they hit close to a mother's heart. Poor little Johnny was about all I could think of when he fell on a broken milk bottle and deeply gashed his right calf, a frightful thing no child should have to endure, nor the parents.

Johnny was of kindergarten age and was playing by the front steps. Fresh milk was delivered each morning from the Berea College Dairy, and we set out the empty bottles for pickup. Somehow, one of them got broken, and there was little Johnny playing close by. Every boy, it seems, must master the art of stilt walking, and with a pair close at hand just beckoning to be ridden, up he went only to slip and fall across the jagged edge of the bottle.

It was a bad cut that probably should have been seen by a doctor, but Taylor had a first aid kit with the sort of quick and immediate battle field requirements the soldiers used. In it was a package of medication designed to be placed directly in severe wounds to stop the bleeding. He poured in the contents as instructed, and Johnny shrieked in pain, the stinging hardly bearable. He was to carry a scar for the rest of his life.

Then there was his playtime friend, the Stivers boy next door, who pelted him with stones one day. They hit him in the face; one leaving its lifelong mark in his forehead just above the right eyebrow. What was a mother to do?

Those sorts of things were not laughable, but locking himself into the bathroom had some humor in it when seen from my perspective well after the fact. It took the fire department, who arrived in full regalia, to get him out through a window. But that occurred only after I climbed out on the back porch roof and took off the screen on the bathroom window. I had tried to make little Johnny understand that all he had to do was to turn the button in the middle of the knob to unlock the door, but he was much too distraught and would only cry louder, screaming, "I can't!"

Those are the sorts of things that remain with a mother long after they are forgotten by the children. All was resolved when Johnny's fright and sobs were quelled in my arms, and the firemen went away with grins on their faces.

When the good jobs at the Ordinance Depot were gone, the pinches began, and the reason I returned to North Carolina was that eventually we couldn't meet payments and lost our High Street house. So, I robbed Peter to pay Paul and eventually moved with my children back to my family's farm.

It was January, 1948, and Taylor had lost his job at the Depot. He took a job as a salesman driving a van like the modern-day Mac Tools trucks and was selling to mechanics and whomever. It wasn't much of a living, but it put food on the table. As if difficult times weren't enough, he developed a huge carbuncle on his right shoulder blade that made it impossible for him to drive the truck.

He was in absolute misery, unable to sleep much and then only on his stomach. Taylor never slept on his stomach, always on his back or sides. He lay on the couch in the living room day and night, suffering, and all I could do was apply hot packs until the carbuncle finally came to a head and drained. Before there were antibiotics to cure infections of this sort, hot packs were about the only way to treat a boil, a stye that the children were forever getting, or carbuncles. That thing had five or six heads in it and left a big hole in the flesh over his shoulder blade that he carried for the rest of his life.

With little income, there was no way to make house payments, pay utility bills, and feed a family, so the house on High Street was rented and we went to live with the Dr. and Mrs. Gabbard. Michaela was nine, and Johnny was seven. It was decided that the two younger children, Charlene, age five, and Alex, all of one year old, would stay with us in the front room of the Gabbard house and that Michaela and Johnny, being the oldest and eating the most, would go to stay with my sister, Lucille, and her husband, H.B., in Charlotte. That was an agonizing thing to do, send off one's children, but it seemed like the only thing to do. Lucille had no children, and she welcomed the chance to have my children in her home.

I did the difficult duty of calling Lucille to tell her to expect Michaela and Johnny at such-and-such a time the next day. Telephone connections were terrible in those days, and Lucille couldn't hear me well enough to know whether to meet a train or a bus at the prescribed time, but she agreed to be there at the appointed time, departing from Lexington, overnight to Charlotte.

The drive from Berea to Lexington to meet the Norfolk & Western train was so difficult for me, sending off two of my children, but for them it was a big adventure. Taylor's younger brother, Junior, drove us to the station. I sat in the middle of the front seat, and André Hanotel, our High Street neighbor from Algiers, sat by the window. Michaela and Johnny had the back seat and must have been

183

tired; it was late in the day and they slept some on the hour-long trip. Departure time was around 10 PM.

I wrote their names and addresses along with Lucille's on baggage tickets and fastened them to their coat lapels so they wouldn't get lost. When we boarded, I entrusted the care of my children to the pleasant conductor, a total stranger. He assured me that he'd see to it that they made the proper connections in Knoxville where they had to change to a Southern Railway train.

Michaela and Johnny took their seats with a little pocket change to buy food from vendors who went through the trains with sandwiches, fruit, and drinks. There I stood waving goodbye to my children, hoping I was doing the right thing, praying silently that they would get through OK.

The train pulled out and was soon out of sight headed south with my Michaela and Johnny on board. That was not a pleasant experience. Michaela told me later that they slept in their passenger coach seats and pulled into the Knoxville station around 6:30 the next morning, and someone, the conductor most likely, made sure that they got on the train to Charlotte.

Michaela was dutifully handling the big sister responsibilities of looking after her little brother and became frightened that they would not know when they got to Charlotte. Each time the train approached a stop along the route, a man walked through the coaches announcing the name of the town, and she couldn't understand a word he said.

She described what she saw but was most fascinated by the soil that had changed color to red while on that last leg of the trip. Someone told her that was because there was lots of iron in the North Carolina clay makaing it red.

They made the entire trip wearing their coats because she was afraid that they would get lost without their baggage tickets telling who they were and where they were going. I was relieved to learn that part had worked well, but two young children traveling by themselves like that....

Finally the man came through the car shouting, "Sha-lott. Next stop."

"Sha-lott!" Michaela, thought. That didn't sound like Charlotte to her, so she wasn't about to move, but the conductor came along and told her this was their stop. He made sure they got off the train at the right place.

In the meantime, Lucille and H.B. had found out that a Greyhound bus was arriving at about the time I had said to expect Michaela and Johnny and that there was also a Southern Railway train arriving at nearly the same time. Because of the bad telephone connection and not being sure which conveyance the children were to arrive on, they decided to split up to make sure one of them met the children. H.B. dropped Lucille off at the train station and he went to the bus station.

I don't know who was happier to see whom, but it was a wonderful reunion there in the train station. And I was relieved to learn that they had arrived just fine. Before long H.B. showed up, having ascertained that the children weren't on the bus, and the four of them gathered whatever luggage they had and drove home.

Lucille and H. B. were living in the upstairs of a private residence at that time. From the front door and up the stairs, their "apartment" consisted of a small alcove at the head of the stairs where Daddy Wolfe's bed sat, left on the landing to the kitchen door, left around the stairs to the attic door, and further left to the bedroom where Lucille and

Lucille, very elegant in 1944

H.B. slept.

There was very little privacy, but it was clean and well-kept, and the Wolfes had laundry privileges, so I suppose it was very nice for the times, especially since they had a private bath.

Michaela's and Johnny's new bed was a roll-away they had borrowed from John and Alice, my parents. It was put in the attic. That was their new home. Times were tough, and while children's problems were mostly overlooked as the adults went about their business making a living, anxieties soon began to show. Both Michaela and Johnny wet the bed; I'm sure they became a terrible trial to Lucille and HB., but fortunately the laundry was nearby.

Michaela, feeling entrusted with her younger brother's care, carried on with a stiff upper lip most of the time, but poor Johnny was dreadfully homesick and missed his Mama terribly. She recalls that he cried himself to sleep every night.

School had been in session for some time, and Lucille took them up the road to the Thomasboro School and enrolled Johnny in second grade and Michaela in fourth.

186

Their previous schools in Kentucky had different curriculums than those in North Carolina, and their classes were almost ready for six-weeks exams when they started. Michaela was horrified: she failed every test that first six-week period. But by the end of the school year both of them had caught up with their classes and were doing well.

Now, looking out for children in those days involved unpleasantries of both the times and notions of adults. Lucille and H.B., believing themselves to be doing the proper thing, insisted that the children take a spring tonic to "clean out your systems." The tonic was castor oil mixed with orange juice and was vile. Michaela, setting the proper example for her little brother, dutifully drank hers, or at least most of it, but Johnny refused. H.B. ended up holding him in a head vise and forcing him to drink by pinching his mouth open. Lucille was begging him to stop, Michaela was crying, but it was to no avail. The head of the family had duties to look after and administering to the children's health was one of them.

Michaela described the "tonic" as doing its job. It cleaned out the pipes giving her the worst case of diarrhea of her entire life!

Lighter moments mixed with homesickness and school tended to make the time pass for my children, I suppose, and some measure of those times became fashioned into their lives. Their circumstances were not what they desired, I am sure, but necessities of the times seem to dictate the arrangement that proved to be more temporary than thought. While living with Lucille and H.B., Johnny got his lengthy nickname: John Henry Hoehandle Jughead Spivins Wet-in-the-Bed Taylor Gabbard Wolfe, Jr. That was H.B.'s lasting contribution to Johnny's young and not so pleasant life away from Mama.

For us, Taylor and me, things continued to worsen. I just couldn't have my children being raised hither and yon by whomever. It was time to pull things together even if it meant pulling apart.

Taylor and I were in the bank in Berea where we came to the end of the road. Ralph Dean, the banker, told Taylor that the bank had given all the considerations they could. He asked that since he was so far behind, what was he going to do? Taylor mentioned that he had a job offer in Louisville managing an all-night restaurant. I didn't see that in my future, or the future for my children, and I told him of a teaching offer I had in North Carolina, but I needed a car to get there. Mr. Dean wanted to know if I could confirm the offer. I used the telephone right there in the bank and called Sam Gentry in Dobson. I told Mr. Gentry that I wanted to come into the North Carolina school system in the coming school year and asked if he had a school for me. "Yes," he said. "We've got a place for you."

So Ralph Dean financed the purchase of my first car. I loaded up my children and what belongings would fit and drove it from Berea back home to Little Richmond. I made the payments of sixty-four dollars a month until it was paid for while teaching in Surry County, North Carolina during 1951 and '52 on a low certificate and soon saw the advantage of finishing college, which I did at Berea College in 1953. Then I began fulltime teaching until I retired.

For the three years between coming to North Carolina and my first teaching job and going back to Berea to finish my last two years of college work, my four children and I lived in the big middle bedroom of the Martin house. There was one big double bed and the infamous rollaway that the children came to loath, and a blocked off fireplace with a wood burning stove. It was crowded, but we made do. Country life was much different than city life, but we were all together.

After completing college at Berea, I taught in Kentucky one year, 1954. I did practice teaching in a little school a good way from Berea. I drove out toward Paint Lick on dirt roads until coming to the foot of a mountain, then turned off and followed the track made by a little stream bed. There was no road. I climbed up the stream bed to the top of the mountain, then went along the top of the ridge until coming to a one-room school house. One teacher taught seven grades.

The children seemed to enjoy the music and art things I did with them, and I enjoyed the children, too. Their lunch program consisted of soup out of cans that was heated on the stove. The bigger boys made the fires and carried out the ashes.

The bigger boys decided that year that they wanted to have a Future Farmers of America project, and they had to have something that they could all participate in. So, after deliberating on various projects, they decided that they wanted to have a pig. Their teacher got in touch with the agriculture teacher at Berea College, Pearl Ayres. His nickname was Pearly, and he found an infant pig for that little school and brought it out to the children. They boarded the pig from house to house and named it Pearly. I don't know what became of the pig, but I feel sure that it probably ended up at a fair with a blue ribbon on it. Pearly was a much loved pig.

That was the year we lost the house on High Street, 1954. I moved back to my family's farm, and Daddy deeded the house I've lived in since to me in 1956. Kentucky didn't have the school system that North Carolina did; there were little 1-teacher and 2-teacher schools scattered hither and yon, much as I described; the pay was not up to what I could get in North Carolina; and the only work that Taylor could get was managing a Louisville restaurant that was open 24-hours a day and had living quarters upstairs. I had children coming into their early teens and just could not bear the thought of them having to work in the kitchen and around the place to keep it going.

I told Taylor that I would go to North Carolina and teach; I didn't ask him for anything; and we lived apart for the next twelve years.

Michaela wanted to finish High School in Berea, and the College had a high school for boarding students that they called Foundation, a preparatory for the college. We made an application to the Foundation School, and immediately, someone from the treasurer's office came out and interviewed her for a job. They wanted smart people who were going to be with them for more than one year. So, Michaela had a job and stayed in Berea as a dormitory student until she graduated.

190

That was where she met L. B. Cox who was from the coal fields of western Virginia. He had lost his mother and was also a dormitory boarding student. His father wasn't able to keep the family together, so L. B. had come to the Foundation School to prepare for college that would continue after high school.

That next year Alex went to live with his father and the family in Dr. Gabbard's house; that was his 5th grade year. He came back to North Carolina as fat as a butter ball. I have never seen anyone put on so much weight; it took us an entire year to get him slimmed down to look normal. He had spent a lot of time serving ice cream out the windows of the "Stand," and by all appearances, he had put as much into himself as he had served customers.

Michaela and Charlene also spent a good deal of time at the "Stand." Open at ten o'clock in the morning and close at midnight every day of the week; not my idea of how children ought to be raised, but they did OK.

I really don't know the origin of the "Stand." I suppose that Dr. Gabbard decided that he needed some kind of small business for his retirement. He was looking ahead, planning I suppose. Possibly, he wasn't feeling too well, and they were already short on money. He and Bell went up into Owsley County and borrowed money from kinfolks to buy the franchise, the trailer made for the ice cream business, the land there just as you leave the Berea city limits on 25E south, and set up business.

The "Stand" on US 25 south of Berea, Kentucky, 1955

The "Stand" was a drive-in "diner" kind of restaurant that served sandwiches and french fries, boxed lunch kinds of things with deep fried chicken, fish and shrimp, all kinds of soft ice cream fixings from milk shakes to you name it, anything a customer might want.

In those days, Route 25 was a main thoroughfare and lots of traffic made the location of the "Stand" a favorite stop for travelers and locals alike, especially in summertime. Vehicles turned off the highway directly into its gravel parking lot, and there they could see the menu listed in large blue letters on its white walls and along the hip of the roof that covered the "diner" part, really a small trailer with big windows and service connections. It took me two days to do the lettering.

That location had horrible water. The well was punched directly into a sulfur stream, and you could see little filaments of black floating throughout the otherwise clear water. It smelled awful, like rotten eggs, but was really cold. Right there on the front of the cinder block storeroom portion of the "Stand" was a water fountain. I painted "Old Faceful" on the wall over it, but hardly anyone drank from that fountain. It had irregular pressure and would literally give you a face full.

I think the business was one of the first drive-in type fast food restaurants that became popular in the 1950s. It featured soft serve ice cream that every one seemed to enjoy so well. I suppose that Dr. Gabbard looked forward to it being a stable and rewarding retirement enterprise for himself, but he didn't live but a short time after it went into business. Ten years later Taylor and his mother, Bell, along with Margaret's daughter JoAnn, and Alex when he stayed with his father, worked it full time.

In 1961 when I went back to college at the University of Kentucky in Lexington, I didn't stay with the Gabbards in Berea; Michaela and I went 50-50 for living quarters, a screened-in back porch and a big up-stairs. She was living with her young family in Lexington, and my accommodations were the sort to be summer only.

After finishing that college bit, I returned to North Carolina with a renewed and improved teaching certificate. It was about then that things really began falling apart for the Gabbard family.

Distance made for little exchange; they were there and we were here in North Carolina. Communications wasn't so quick in those days, and we didn't have much contact, anyway. They ended up having to give up the "Stand;" JoAnn married and moved to Cincinnati. Taylor and his mother moved to Elizabethtown near Louisville where he looked for work. Soon, both died there, and JoAnn was soon to follow. She died during a severe attack of asthma - her heart just stopped beating at age 26. Her children went to live with their father's family in Kansas City, Missouri. Such a sad end to a family.

Front yard artist;
Studebaker, pine tree, and the path to the big house,
back home in Little Richmond 1955

Mothers

L ife in the Martin house in Little Richmond and in the
Gabbard house in Bereawas as different as the
people these homes revolved around. Michaela and I
spent some time musing about these ladies, and since we
had experiences with them at different times, combining our
recollections painted an entertaining picture.

My mother, Alice, and Taylor's mother, Bell, were
totally different people from very different backgrounds.
Mama was a nervous, energetic person who just couldn't let
a minute pass without doing something. She almost always
had at least two projects going at the same time, and burned
food was the usual outcome.

Bell was also energetic, but she could keep her
attention focused on one thing at a time and then go on to
the next. The most visible aspect of her appearance was that

the first finger of her right hand was missing, gone completely to the knuckle at her palm. I seem to recall that she told me that she chopped it off with an axe while chopping wood as a child. That's probably right, because her mother, America, died when Bell was about 11 yrs. old, and she had to drop out of school to become the mother in her family. I don't recall what her father, Squire Combs, did, but the impression that I got was that life in Owsley County was, for the most part, difficult.

By being curtailed so early in her life, Bell's education suffered terribly, resulting in spelling that was rudimentary at best, and she wrote the way she talked, "allus" for always, for example. And because she couldn't properly grip a writing utensil, her writing was a challenge in the best of times. I suspect that her penmanship skills similarly suffered due to lack of development.

Alice, on the other hand, was well educated and refined with a family legacy far from the back woods, and she bitterly resented being stuck way out in the country on the farm. She lived for Sundays that gave her what little time she had to socialize. That was her day off, and she took complete advantage of it to visit, even if she had to walk to a neighbor's house, which she frequently did.

In one respect these two mothers were identical: their houses were immaculate. Mama had a greater challenge because the farm had a dirt road running in front of the house, and everybody coming in carried dirt in on their feet. But she never let a day go by without sweeping, mopping, dusting and making beds. She also had to make time to milk cows twice daily, make butter and cottage cheese in addition to cooking three square meals a day on a wood-fired stove, no matter how hot the weather. Both mothers raised big gardens and "put up" food in glass jars for the winter.

Bell wasn't much of a socializer, but she had friends nearby she could walk to and visit with during the afternoon, then be back home to prepare the evening meal on her electric range that was the centerpiece of her rather well equipped kitchen.

While our mothers tended to their houses and families, the fathers had other business. Daddy traveled sales routes and was gone for extended periods of time when I was little. When he gave up selling and became a farmer around the time of the second war, he was out working long days, sun up to sun down.

Living on the fringe of a town, Chester did his dentistry, tended to his garden and participated in Lodge activities. His garden lay between the back of the house and barn that was the long branch of the "L" shaped property while the other branch went down Elder Street to Rachel and "Uncle Mike's" house. The barn was for no more than one cow kept for milk, and milking was Bell's job. At the back corner of the screen porch near the cement steps leading up from the basement grew a large paw-paw tree. It was a curiosity to the children and bore edible fruit loaded with seeds, and it tended to draw bees to the paw-paws that fell and lay rotting on the ground.

Chester used to sit under a tree in the back yard with his rifle in hand and shoot crows that raided his corn. This was well before crows were included on the endangered species list as a relative of the raven, of course, and that's a good thing because he was dead eye dick with that rifle.

Bell had a ritual in her housekeeping. Every morning after the breakfast were washed, she'd start by making beds that required fluffing up feather mattresses, and then the scatter rugs in the living room were carried out to the front porch to be swept off and dusted. A dust mop was run over all the hardwood floors before the rugs were brought back inside, and then all the furniture was dusted with a cloth. She also had a talent for raising African Violets, and she looked after them once everything else was done.

Wash day saw both mothers up to their elbows in suds, but Mama did her laundry in a big pot or in a tub on the back porch, after which everything was hung out to dry on the clotheslines just beyond the well between the bottom of the steps from the porch and the barn.

Bell did her washing in the basement. She had a wringer washer with tubs for rinsing, and her laundry was hung out to dry on clotheslines in the back yard, too. Mama washed clothes in water that was wound up out of the well a bucketful at a time, then carried up the steps, into the house and poured into big pots on the wood stove for heating. Later, in the late 1940s, running water was brought into the house, and that simplified things quite a lot.

Bath time for us children was also quite different. Here on the farm, we mostly sponged off with a wash cloth and a pan of water, but on Saturday night we did, indeed, get into a big zinc tub that was brought into the kitchen and placed in front of the kitchen stove for warmth. A lot of water had to be drawn and heated to fill that big tub, and as children, even my own children later on, there would be some spilt water and suds that required running a mop over the floor afterward.

Bell, on the other hand, had both hot and cold running water and an inside bath with a tub, plus a shower in the basement. Old habits die hard, though, and Chester only bathed on Saturday nights. Taylor often remarked, "I just can't understand how he can put clean clothes on every day and not take a bath!"

Our heating supply on the farm was, for the most part, a big wood pile. Daddy chopped planks or split wood for heating and cooking. The house had functional fireplaces, but they didn't provide much heat - most went straight up the chimneys. So, they ended up being blocked off during the winter and stayed that way for the most part. In the rooms that were occupied, a wood burning Franklin type stove was the only source of heat.

The rooms that we occupied served as bedroom and living room, and everybody huddled around the source of heat on cold mornings to wash up and get dressed. The rest of the house, except for the kitchen, had no heat, so we usually slept under several quilts that Mama had made by hand. Later, in a move to ease the amount of work required to heat the room Mama and Daddy shared, a pile of coal replaced the wood pile, so the axe spent a lot more time sitting unused in the shed.

Bell had central heat. First it was coal, so somebody had to keep the furnace stoked and the cinders taken out. Then it was fuel oil. That was a real luxury! Warm air flowing throughout the house, each room warm and cozy, and nothing to do but keep the oil tank filled. But, for hot water, a little wood burning stove beside the furnace had to be stoked up, and that took some time before a warm shower was available; not an inconvenience, really, it just required a little planning ahead. That was a minor inconvenience considering that she didn't have to heat water on the kitchen stove like my mother did.

Thoughtful designers of those wood burning stoves

had them built with a cavity located beside the firebox; that was the hot water supply, and if kept filled, hot water was always available. The farm had to be tended to on cold winter days just as any other day, and a tea kettle always on a burner steaming away provided moisture to make the house more pleasant, not to mention a hot cup of Sanka or Postum to warm ourselves.

Both mothers kept a few chickens, so there were always fresh eggs for breakfast - no worries about cholesterol in those days! Bell was an excellent cook, a talent she passed on to Taylor, and not having learned much of the culinary arts as I grew up, he taught me how to cook. Because of the relentless pace that the house, farm and family presented to Mama, she was never much of a cook, unfortunately, but our table seemed to always have takers pulling up chairs.

Grace was said three times a day at our table. In Kentucky we didn't return thanks and dug right in. Mama usually said grace at breakfast and lunch, and I can't remember how it went, but it was usually a short repeat. Daddy said grace at the evening meal, and here's how his went:

"Heavenly Father, we wish to thank you for the
day and for its blessings. We ask that you
forgive our sins and save us for Christ's sake.
In Christ's name we pray... Amen"

Just before the "Amen," he always sniffed. Just a habit, I guess, but I'll always wonder if there was any significance to be attached to it.

As Johnny, Charlene and Alex came along, they

were expected to help out on the farm. Every morning, on went the boots and the troop headed by Daddy, then me, then my children headed for the barn to milk the cows. Of course there wasn't time to bathe afterwards, and we all went to school smelling like cow.

Before he went off to the Navy after high school, Johnny raised a crop or two of tobacco with Daddy, and he made some money at it, enough to buy himself his first car. His blue Ford coupe was seen parked on the side of 268 on a few occasions, the victim of another broken clutch, but he did pretty well at keeping his car going.

Charlene wasn't much for farming and had some stomach problems that required less strenuous activities. And Alex always seemed to find something else to do, or just not be ready when we had to head to the barn, then he wouldn't show up for miling and went off to wait for the bus out of range of questions.

Then there was the evening milking. The cows had to be called up and fed, and we had to do the milking while they were feeding, otherwise they got restless.

Bucket after bucket of milk was strained twice a day and went into gallon size glass jars that kept the dining room refrigerator full. By the next day, the cream had separated from the milk, and, that done, churning turned it into butter.

Bell, on the other hand, went to her telephone and called up the grocery store located on the street with Boone Tavern and gave her list. Within an hour or two the delivery van pulled up, and groceries were delivered. It seems that most of the time, some item or other wasn't quite what she wanted, and that evoked some stern words for the grocer who was supposed to know what she wanted. After all, she had been buying her groceries from him a long enough.

Market day in Elkin, usually Friday morning, brought a flurry of activity from Mama who thoroughly enjoyed socializing with all the farmers who brought their goods to the vacant lot under the bridge that spanned the Yadkin to Jonesville. This was Elkin's farmer's market. Her fresh butter was squeezed into wooden molds and pressed to expel as much milk as possible, then each one was wrapped in wax paper making 1-pound portions. Each molding had a flower pattern impressed into it, and along with eggs, cookies and other products of her kitchen, she anxiously awaited the arrival of Kizzie Martin from Salem Fork. These two old ladies going to town in Kizzie's yellow DeSoto were a sight to behold. Mama just couldn't seem to get going quickly enough.

Mama never had the luxury and pleasure of the amenities that Bell enjoyed. Farm life was quite different than city life and left little time to pursue the kind of life she wanted most. Even a standard amenity today, a bathroom. It was later in her life, by the time my children were teenagers, when indoor plumbing was installed in the Martin house. That came with the addition of electric heating about seven decades after the house had been built.

Our mothers had done the best they could with what life gave them, and, quicker than I ever imagined, I found myself doing the same, being a mother and making do. Michaela and her hard working husband, L.B., do the bulk of the farming now, so the legacy of John and Alice continues on the same land and in the same house that they knew.

As it sometimes does, life dealt them a harsh blow by taking their only child, Bradley, just before his fourth birthday. Johnny and his wife, Pat, raised a boy and a girl;

Charlene and her husband,
Ron, raised two girls; Alex
and his wife, Mary, raised
two boys; Nick and his
wife, Darlene, have two
daughters about grown now.
Lots of mothers on my tree.
    Me? I garden a little
when its warm, and when
it's cold I perch by my central heat just meanwhiling.

Changes

By the 1950s, Burch Station was just a shadow of its previous existence. Times had changed. The big warehouse building was gone; the Station house, too, along with the foreman's bungalow. The little store had been taken down and rebuilt; a four room cottage with a metal roof now stood on John Martin's land adjacent to Vance Burch's place. This was my house where I raised my children.

Howell Carter's big garage stood alone by the highway at its doorstep. State Route 268 had long since been paved, the old road forgotten, and cars whizzed by incessantly. If their occupants took notice at all, they saw an old structure increasingly showing its age but revealing none of its history.

It stands today, lonely, its past largely forgotten.

Quiet.

The people long since gone.

After three decades, mail was no longer a railroad service - our little post office, Rusk, closed in 1951. Trucks now rolled the highways providing service where the iron horse was once king. No one speaks of the sand clay road any more, and only remnants of the old road bed running in front of this house and on by the John Martin house to Snow Creek remain. There the supports of the Snow Creek bridge stand today, well up the Mitchell River toward the Ashburn place, its steel long since scrapped for the war.

A search for the mill's concrete footings might turn up hints of the once-upon-a-time focus of the Mitchell River, where Buster tied up his mule and "Gee" ground flour, meal, and feed. What remained of the dam lasted a few years more. Then, the water's eternal flow returned to unobstructed rippling down the rocky face of the granite cap it had exposed eons ago.

Route 268's Mitchell River bridge is a wide, modern, concrete thing now, but if you look though the trees on down the river, the railroad trestle can be seen back into time. That old triangulated Warren Truss still does its duty for the freights that run occasionally, and with a little imagination, you might picture that very kind of structure, a 1-lane bridge with heavy plank flooring covered in asphalt, as the highway bridge of yesterday's 268.

And just picture a hot summer day with my boys, Johnny, Alex and Nick, swinging from long grapevines out over the cold Mitchell water and dropping into it with mighty splashes having the times of their lives.

Hush! It's coming!

Last passenger run to Burch Station - only freight from now on.

One little boy waited expectantly in his mother's arms; a grandson of John and Alice Martin waited for his first ride on the choo-choo. Most of the small group that had gathered for the occasion felt deprived and had a sense of loss, although they had rarely paid any attention to the train. Change was in the air, and it wasn't seen as good.

Cars parked around the station showed how people chose to travel; the train was from an earlier time, and whatever was being lost would soon be forgotten.

Just as Buster's excitement had been the mark of that time, little Alex's excitement was of the new era; trains would be little more than an interest in his life of cars, not the life blood of the previous generation, my generation.

His excitement brought back memories. Remarks were exchanged that the little boy did not appreciate.

"All trucks now. Faster, faster, everything's faster."

"Yep, the world's in an awful hurry."

"The railroad was new when your Grandpa sold fertilizer out of a box car here. Everybody came from miles around."

"And we brought buckets of blackberries to sell - they poured'em into a barrel for wine makin'."

"Ride to Elkin for 15-cents. Up in the morning on the 'Up Train,' back on the 'Down Train' in the afternoon."

The conductor beamed at young Alex. "Going to ride with us?"

As the child's little head bobbed with agreement, the engineer picked up the boy and toted him up to the engine. There the engineer kept his romper attired assistant for the six mile run while the conductor visited in the passenger car.

"When I was a child," I mused, "we rode the 'Down Train' along the river as far as Donnaha where we met the East Bend mailman. He took passengers along with mail bags to the post office. At the station, the conductor sang out his little ditty,

> "All off for Mt. Airy-y-y,
>   Pilot Mountain,
>   Walnut Co-o-o-ve.
>   Don't forget your little packages."

Everyone just smiled.

Change for East Bend, too. The mailman always had room for us and talked a blue streak.

"Your Grampa's got a fine store... I remember your Mama waiting on customers... before she married that mountain man...."

But there was no one who remembered but me. Had it been just thirty years?

Family Stories

Alex had become enamored with the Sears-Roebuck catalog and sidled up to Gramma Flora, Little Granny to the grandkids, and asked if she might have one hundred dollars he could have to buy the things he'd seen on page after page. He had big ambitions, but that much money in the early-1950s had considerable buying power. Gramma Flora got a hearty chuckle telling that story.

We were five generations then. I was in the middle with my mother, Alice, and her mother, Flora, the older folks, then my eldest, Michaela, with her only child, Bradley, in her arms. We made a fine picture, a moment captured in time, but change quickly removed the ends of our five, old age taking my grandmother and a car taking my grandson.

Gramma Flora frequented the John Martin home for lengthy stays; she had no home of her own. So, she was a part of my life from the time I was little when Mama and I visited in East Bend to her passing well into my adult life. By then, wheelchair bound, always in a black dress, aged, white hair always pulled up into a bun, Gramma Flora was just the shadow of the refined lady she had been with a fine house and big store in East Bend.

Grandma Flora c. 1940

By then, both Mama and Gramma Flora were of the older set, both very independent, and perhaps with a little envy thrown in; Mama had means that her mother didn't.

Mama was a dynamo, always keeping several projects going at the same time. She rarely sat down during the day except for meals. Visitors provided a wonderful opportunity for a break in the monotonous routine of work, work, work, and the children had better behave or pay the consequences with a severe tongue-lashing.

Gramma Flora was homeless after W. A.'s death because he left his property to the Church with no provision for Flora to use it during her lifetime. In a most un-Christian action, the church elders evicted her. From that day until her death years later, she lived with one or another of her children, often moving, but she spent most of her time with Alice, who was in her late 60s.

It was hard to tell which was the older when the two old ladies got to sniping at each other, and when matters reached the boiling point, Daddy knew it was time to call Woodrow, Flora's youngest son, and ask him to take Flora home with him for a while.

On one such occasion, Woodrow came on a Sunday, which was Mama's only day of rest. She took full advantage of it to sit on the porch and visit after Sunday School and church services. Somebody always showed up, usually family members but often neighbors who dropped by. After an hour or so, Woodrow indicated that it was time to head back home to East Bend. Flora was dressed in her Sunday best, complete with hat, and she was ceremoniously placed in the front passenger seat while her luggage was stowed in the trunk.

These two old ladies hadn't been speaking for several days by this time, and it was obvious by Flora's up-turned nose and set jaw that she was glad to be leaving. She sat in stony silence, staring straight ahead while Woodrow said his goodbyes to Alice and John.

Nobody ever left without saying, "Y'all come on with us, now!" because it was the polite thing to do, whether it was meant or not. But when Woodrow asked, "Why don't you come on with us, Alice?" he was stunned when she replied, "Well, I just think I will."

To everybody's amazement, Mama went inside the house and picked up a suitcase packed and ready, put on her shawl, carried the suitcase to the trunk, and proceeded to

210

climb into the back seat right behind her mother, who by this time was in a state of high dudgeon. After all, it was HER who was supposed to be leaving, not Alice!

Gramma Flora tossed her head and sniffed, "Well, I do declare! You just can't go anywhere without having to take your children along!"

Story telling was a big part of Sunday afternoon porch-sitting at the Martin house. Daddy might get out his banjo and plink some, but if it happened to be raining and the children were confined to the porch, he had stories to tell. The glider swing on the side porch had been our loco-motive when Ben, Lucille and I played on it as children, and now my children found the same fascination. But after a while, even that source of fun wore thin.

Among Daddy's favorites were the panther and snake tales that enthralled the children and gave everyone apprehensive prickles. It seems that a circus train had wrecked. Just when wasn't said, just years ago, and some of the animals got loose. The giant snake slithered off to who knows where, and the panther added its shrill cry to the night.

"That big cat sounded just like a woman screaming," he'd say to big eyes and open mouths entranced in his story-telling. "Scary feeling... Always at night." And of course he wasn't quite sure whatever happened to the ferocious panther, it might still be out there in the woods somewhere, all the more reason for children to be in the house at night.

The snake? That was another thriller; the slithery thing nearly got him, too. You can imagine the looks on the grandchildren's faces. There he was, walking the branch fence checking that the barbed wire was in place when something rustled in the thick, summertime foliage overhead.

Daddy had a way of telling matter-of-fact tales so convincingly that they just had to be true, and every imagination leaped to the vision of the beady eyed giant laying in wait, flicking its tongue at the dinner approaching below. It was his sixth sense about danger than caused him to hesitate just at the right moment when that creature hurled itself out of the trees toward its prey, just missing, and landing with a great SPLASH! in the branch. Startled at the sight of such a gigantic snake, Daddy just stood there and watched it slither off into the woods.

"That thing was as long as my truck and as big around as my leg, " he emphasized with his hands spanning just above the knee. "Biggest snake anybody ever heard about around here."

Well, a few days later, that snake showed up again. Daddy had a couple of colored men ploughing the bottom, and one of them stopped to rest in the shade by a sizable creek. He nearly stumbled himself to death getting back to his friend to tell him of the giant snake he saw coiled up on a flat rock in the middle of the creek. The two of them investigated quietly and found it to be so.

"One big coil after another covered that rock, as big as a hogshead," Daddy emphasized drawing his outstretched hand round and round. "Big snake. Giant snake."

Now, ordinarily, snakes were the sorts of things that drew big eyes and a turn-and-run, but this one was so big that it offered up a different set of possibilities. They decided to capture it. That would make them the talk of the town. And since there was no town nearby, they'd take it to Elkin, North Wilkesboro maybe, wherever the glory of being the giant snake catchers followed them.

Imagine that! Here they were peeking through the weeds at a snake that was probably stronger than the two of them put together, and they were already savoring the stories they would tell. That snake just kept on sunning. All they had to do was catch it.

Perhaps being a circus snake rather used to people made it an easier to catch than one in the wild, but catch it they did. And they did it with sticks and ropes and a big bag. Caught that snake! You've never seen a couple of prouder men in your life, and it didn't take away from their glory that it was killed in the process. On the contrary, the two of them were clearly masters of the giant creature.

So, they went to town. They tied that snake to the back bumper of their car and paraded through main street stopping here and there to tell their story. It was a proud, proud day.

The Little Richmond school house was the center of life during the school days of two or three generations of children around here. It was one of many built throughout the state, the result of an early building program that closed lots of little schools in favor of larger consolidated schools for a region. One just like it was built in North Elkin and still stands, but the Little Richmond School was cleared away several years ago, maybe in the late 1970s.

All the elementary schools in Surry County were laid out the same way, built of brick with lots of big classroom windows that give fine lighting. The rectangular floor plan with classrooms around a large, open auditorium with a large stage at the back of the building turned out to produce quite a chimney effect. Hardwood floors were cleaned and oiled regularly, and when one of these buildings went up in flames, it went in a hurry. That's what happened to Little Richmond.

I'm sure there are many saddened hearts around here when former students of our school look upon the bare ground where it once stood and recall many childhood memories it provided.

When Ben was away in the Navy during World War II, there were months on end when he wasn't heard from. All the correspondence was censored so military positions wouldn't be given away, and sometimes mail was just slow. Mama worried about Ben constantly.

One summer day when Michaela was playing in the front yard and Mama was in the side yard hanging out the wash, Michaela looked up the road and saw a man in uniform walking toward the house. She recognized him. Well, like any excited child, she starting shouting as loud as she could, "It's Ben! Ben's come home. Gramma, come quick - it's Ben!"

Poor Mama dropped the laundry and ran as fast as she could to the front yard calling, "Ben! Ben!" with every breath. By this time he was in the yard and started to go to Mama, but she fell to her knees right at the corner of the house and walked the last few feet to him on her knees. Ben was embarrassed, Michaela could tell, and she was amazed

Ben, a sailor during WW-2

to see her Grandmother blubbering over him like that, but her boy was home and he was alive and that was all Mama cared about.

Before the war, H. B. Wolfe had met Lucille and carried on correspondence with her while she worked in New Jersey. I think she shared an apartment with Lora and Joyce Martin. He was in the North Africa campaign fighting Germany's infamous "Desert Fox," General Rommel, and I believe he proposed to her in one of his letters.

They were married soon after he got out of the service, and they made their home in Charlotte where Lucille worked for Duke Power and he became a brick mason. For newlyweds, though, his job took him away from home too often for too long, and, like Mama, Lucille was afraid of staying alone. So, he became a Charlotte taxi driver. They never had children; maybe they couldn't, maybe they wanted it that way, I don't know. That was the sort of thing you didn't ask people about in those days.

H. B.'s father, Daddy Wolfe, was diabetic and lived with them for quite a long time before his death in the early 1950s, I think. Daddy Wolfe had several surgical procedures to remove gangrenous toes, then feet, then part of a leg, and finally the whole leg so that he was bed-ridden. Lucille was his nurse, and I never knew her to complain.

Lucille was a pretty woman and very thrifty. Taylor once said, "Lucille could take the bus to town for 10-cents each way, shop, and still bring home change from a dollar." Maybe so, but I'm sure that she and H. B. didn't have much money, so she probably had to play it close to the vest.

When Michaela and Johnny lived with Lucille and H. B. the winter of 1947, I wasn't able to send any money for their support. Taylor supplied nothing in terms of child support, and I wasn't working, so I had no income. Keeping two children had to be a burden, both financial and emotional, but they never complained. It was, I suspect, both a welcomed opportunity to have children in the house, and an unwelcome expense. But we all got by.

Come Mother's Day that year, and I was pleased to no end to get a phone call from Lucille and my children. Phone service wasn't very good, and long distance connections were awful - lots of static with the sound fading in and out. Michaela, age 9, was first to wish me Happy Mother's Day, then she gave the phone to Johnny, age 7, for him to do the same, but all he could do was cry.

It might have been three weeks later when I arrived in Charlotte from Kentucky to collect my children. Alex was

216

just a babe in arms and Charlene was a toddler. Finally, I had all my children together, but Taylor had lost his job at the Blue Grass Ordnance Depot, and we had to rent the High Street house while living with Dr. and Mrs. Gabbard. That didn't last long.

It wasn't long after that when H. B. asked if Michaela could come live with them; Lucille needed help. She hadn't been there long when, one evening, Lucille fell to pieces with her first nervous breakdown. The next day, Taylor and I arrived to pick up Michaela, then drove up to the farm to tell Mama and Daddy. All Daddy could say was, "She's crazy as a betsy bug. The only thing to do is send her to Morganton."

That's just what happened, of course, and she was given electric shock treatments. Lucille was in and out of the mental hospital in Morganton several times and never fully recovered from her initial breakdown. She would sit on the porch all day gazing out who knows where while slowly twirling a strand of her hair. Something had happened; something strange that kept her quietly in her world that was no longer connected to the real world around her. In later years she seemed to have resolved her situation and was as alert as normal, but the cumulative effect of several decades of tranquilizers left her with hands that shook uncontrollably.

H. B. died in 1982 of congestive heart failure. Lucille stayed on in their house for a year or two, and one of her neighbors came and slept in the house with her so she wouldn't be alone at night. I drove down fairly often to check on her and to visit, and Ben and Sadie went every other weekend to clean and "do" for Lucille. After that, she went into to a nursing home in Banner Elk where she died after some time of sister and brother looking after her affairs.

Our community has a fascinating past and an energetic future with everyone on the go. Things have changed, that's for sure, but some things remain. Up 268 a mile or so stands the Little Richmond Baptist Church as it has for about as long as anyone can remember. It's a fine brick church that has been the focus of who knows how many preachings, saved souls, baptisms, marriages, and burials. Its predecessor, the old church beyond

My last child, Nicholas, just six, and Mama on the steps of the Little Richmond Baptist Church Mother's Day, 1959

Daddy's barn on the old road to the Mitchell River, moved long ago, as I've told about earlier, but its graveyard remains in the edge of our pasture across from the barn.

When I was little, there were lots of stories about those people buried there, all sorts of scary tales told mostly by older children to scare younger ones. But make no mistake; we talked quite a lot among ourselves about the mysterious aspects of life and death that patch of ground held.

One story was about a wandering, delirious young woman in a thin dress who came out of nowhere on a rainy night and died a day or two later with no one learning anything about her, not even her name. Whether or not that's true no one knows, but it's the kind of story that got handed down from generation to generation with due respect for the "lost" people of that graveyard. All the headstones are slab rock without markings, so there's nothing to mark the existence of these people. We just don't know anything about any of them, where they came from, where they lived, not a single name, not a single homeplace. But what that graveyard does tell us is that people were around here long before us. My guess is that it goes back to the original settlers in this part of the country, certainly well back into the 1800s, maybe the 1700s.

Life on the Martin farm was about like all the other farms around us, mostly work from dawn to dusk, but we lived the farm life as well. We were filled with memories. I suppose that's about what life amounts to.

Daddy had strong notions about most things, but he was the quiet type and kept plodding along. When the  fields or orchard or barn or cows or whatever else in a never ending list of things to do weren't calling too loudly, he took time out to do things that could be described as playful. Many

Daddy and his little wagon c. 1950

times when visitors came with children, he'd hitch up his little calf-drawn wagon and let them ride. He became rather noted for that bit of extravagance, as children got to asking if they could ride, and usually he'd oblige. There really wasn't much riding done, the calves mostly wandered about eating as they went. But it was fun and entertaining.

High Street

About 1951 or '52, Andreé Hanotel and her mother, Mimi, moved into the house next door to us on High Street. They were from Algiers. Andreé was a fabric designer who had come to this country after the war under the refugee program in which a foreign person desiring to come to the United States was taken under the care of a family or group of citizens who were willing to look after the refugee for five years. During that time, the refugee learned how America worked, then they could apply for citizenship. Andreé had done just that and had become a US citizen.

With her skill at weaving, she got a job with Churchill Weavers, a Berea College industry. She would sit down at a loom and set up the warp to lay out the pattern that the weaver would then run with the cross-ways threads to make the design come out as she had designed.

She arrived first, and after she got settled in, she sent for her mother. I never knew Madam Hanotel's given name, she was just Mimi to me, and quite an elegant lady. Their possessions were shipped on the same boat that Mimi came on, and it was quite interesting to see the dismantling of the single, large wooden crate that contained everything.

The bed supports had been laid flat; there wasn't a set of spring or mattress as we think of them. Up went the head, foot and side rails, and then rope cording was run back and forth to hold the mattress. The mattress was handmade. On the farm, we had always stuffed mattresses with straw, but she stuffed hers with newspapers.

The way that was done was by taking a single sheet of newspaper and loosely crumpling it, then stuffing it into a corner of the empty mattress and so on until the mattress was filled. When she got through, she stitched closed the opening, and laid the mattress on the rope supports. And when the bed was made, it looked like any other bed.

In the bedroom furnishings there was also a beautiful wooden wardrobe with two doors, each with a full mirror along with a fairly high kind of chest of drawers with two little raised sections with little drawers, one on either side, probably for jewelry.

For the living room, they had bought American style couches, but in their shipment came leather ottomans, large cushions, emptied and flat. She stuffed them with newspaper, and scattered them around a beautiful hammered copper tray as large as a table top. It was huge and had a fluted edge, all with a beautiful pattern hammered into it.

An Arabian coffer service was also a thing of beauty. Andreé said that everybody in Algiers had that type of coffee service, quite different than anything I had seen.

In the dining room was a table with six chairs. The legs had been taken off the table, wrapped and laid flat with the top, and the chairs had been cleverly packaged together as 6 and 9 combinations. I had never seen such a beautiful pattern of weaving as was in those chair seats and backs. It was a natural straw color so beautifully done by hand. Everything came in that one big container.

Charlene has mentioned that her most memorable recollection of Mimi was that when she was all dressed up, her nipples were suitably colored and showed through openings in her dress. I don't recall noticing Mimi's attire, but French bras of that style worn under a sheer blouse was the kind of thing I have seen, a fairly becoming thing in those days, though.

Charlene was the only one of my children to receive a nickname that stuck. Wouldn't you know that Michaela got shortened to Mike and Charlene became Charlie, so all my children got boy names, but Andreé and Mimi carried on with the dubbing of "Cookie" that Charlene received from the nurses when she was born in Charlotte. That was because Dagwood and Blondie in the funnies had a baby girl, named Cookie when Charlene was born, and "Cookie" both of them have been ever since.

Mimi was quite a lady, but with a stubborn streak. The only thing that she did that didn't set well in the community was that, if she wanted to, she mowed her lawn on Sunday. Well, that upset the Rev. Mylum who lived directly behind the Hanotel house in the parsonage that was located behind the Baptist church. The church faced the main street, looking south, that ran through Berea. From the side walk in front of the Hanotel house to the sidewalk of the main street in front of the church spanned the entire block. In fact, the pastor put it into his sermon, about working on Sunday, and when word got back to Mimi that he was preaching against her choice of working on the Sabbath, she just snorted and went ahead doing what she pleased.

Mimi wasn't proficient in English, and whenever something came up that she didn't understand, she would come over tugging whoever was the source of the misunderstanding along with her and get me to assist. When the postman, for instance, brought a letter that had to be signed for, Mimi reached for it happily only to have the postman pull it back. He told her she had to sign her name for it, but she didn't understand. So, she took him by the shirt and pulled him to my house. I told her in her language to sign, then the light dawned, and she got her letter.

After a year or so there, Mimi and Andreé moved to Newark. That was about a year before I left Berea during the summer of '54. I remember when they were packing up; I took food over to them because their kitchen was already packed, and we said our farewells over my morsels. Later Andreé married, and I have a couple of her letters that I have preserved. I was very fond of Andreé. She was a clever, hard working woman, and quite beautiful.

On the other side of our house, on the corner of High Street, lived the Huddlestons. He was the freight agent for the L&N railroad and used his garage that adjoined our back yard for storing freight in transit and for heating coal for his home. Well, one day I looked out and smoke was just billowing from that garage. I ran for the phone and called the fire department while Andreé hooked up the water hose and put the fire out. It wasn't much of a fire, really, more smoke than anything, but with much clanging and sirens sounding the firemen soon arrived to find the damage to be little more than a smoked up refrigerator. And there was little Alex scared about the commotion and saying that he just wanted to see what coal looked like when it burned.

Alex at eight

Across the street lived Mamie Potts. She was a maiden lady who lived with her aged father. He didn't see very well and let it be known that he couldn't read for himself and that he was always glad to have people read to him - hint, hint. So, from time to time, he would wander over with something in hand, and I would oblige.

He once told me that the wonderful thing about his daughter was that she wanted to improve herself but didn't have any money or backing. So, she took a correspondence course on how to play the piano. The lessons came through the mail, and she worked out the theory part of music with her fingers on a table top keyboard, a cardboard strip simulating a piano keyboard that came with the lessons. When she got to the point that she was ready for a real piano, she went to the Methodist church to play theirs.

Mamie became very proficient, and the church

225

invited her to be their keyboard person. She held that job for years while she taught any of the local children who were beginners at the piano, and I think she must have done a very good job because there were students coming and going all the time. She did well enough to provide for herself and her father, too. And, I suspect, she purchased the house as well.

Remember, this was before there was any government support for the retired. She did it all herself, and was a good neighbor.

And, of course, Mamie would quarrel at Alex every time he held her cat up by its tail making the poor thing squall and clamor to be set loose. She should have nettled his little legs for doing that. Mamie was a good soul.

High Street wasn't really a street. It was more of a court that turned off the main street coming down hill slightly then making a ninety degree left for a straight stretch passing several houses on either side, then another ninety degree left up hill and back to the main street. Beyond it, the hill dropped away, oh, I don't know how sharply but quite a sudden drop.

High Street was a wide, shallow, wide "U," and the curve by the Huddlestons near our house collected sand that washed across it when rain runoff flowed down the street. Once Alex, in only summer shorts, came barreling down the street on his sister's bicycle, lost it and slid along the asphalt and sand giving himself a thorough scraping from head to foot.

With five children, there were lots of those sorts of occasions that required Mama to get out the alcohol and cotton balls and perform first aid.

In the back yard of our house stood a monument

A party in our back yard on High Street, 1953.
That's me talking as Nick sleeps in the buggy.
Note the monument commemorating
the founding of Berea College in 1855.

that said something like, "On this spot in the study of John
G. Fee, Berea College was founded." That was in 1855 or
so. Our back yard was a big one good for children to play
in, and in the back it had a brick picnic grill for cooking
outside. The grill was up against the parsonage fence, and
the pastor's children, a boy and a girl, and my children
played together.

One rainy morning, the pastor's wife told the children to go in the back of the church and play in the Sunday
School rooms. They were equipped with crayons and paper
and similar things. Presently, a little parade went up the
street; the Mylum children and the Gabbard children, every
one with money in their hands, were going to buy candy.
They all came back happily slurping their choices, and the
pastor's wife discovered that the Sunday offering had been

227

Nicholas at eleven

left in the plates where the children had helped themselves and were enjoying the proceeds.

Another time, the pastor had been painting some object with red paint and hadn't gotten finished when he was called away for some reason. Well, there sat that bucket of red inviting and so enticing that when the pastor returned, there on the white wall on the back of the parsonage was swipe after swipe of red paint. I think each one of the children had taken turns in attempting to paint the parsonage red making quite a clean up job.

My children were forever with the pastor's children or his children were with mine, especially when I made doughnuts. When I baked bread, I always put a "preacher pan" full in the oven and took it over to the Mylums, O. B. and Dixie, who were the nicest folks. My children often sat at their table, all good memories I'm sure.

After we left Berea, I learned some years later that Dixie was teaching at the High School. She had a Master's degree and well qualified. The pastor, having met with bad fortune, was no longer with the church. While driving on an icy road, his car had slid and killed a child. It was told to me that he never recovered from the incident.

Across from the church was a theater that my children often went to for 10-cent matinee movies. Beside it was an old hotel. Taylor's mother, Bell, told me that they came to Berea from Owsley County on the promise of work at the college. Both Taylor's father, Chester, and his grandfather, "Uncle Mike" were carpenters, and I recall once when the head nurse at the hospital showed me the doors saying that "Uncle Mike" had perfectly hung every door in the hospital. He was a master carpenter.

Then, when Chester decided to become a dentist, he went off to school in Louisville, and Bell with two children at the time moved in to live with Rachel and "Uncle Mike." Bell got a job cooking in this hotel. That was 1915, I think. I believe the hotel didn't make it beyond the '50s.

A building or two toward the college from the theater was the Masonic Lodge building. Taylor spent a lot of time playing cards in the Lodge.

As a family, we never did anything socially. I don't recall that we ever went to the movies as a family or to church as a family. During the war when there wasn't much to do, we had little children and babysitters were unknown. He played cards at the Lodge, or the men got together to play cards at our house.

Later, while we lived on High Street, Taylor's younger brother, Junior, and his wife and baby came over frequently. Our children were bigger and slept upstairs, and we put their little boy to bed in our bedroom. We adults played canasta half the night. We'd pop corn, and once in a while when it got late, we might brew a pot of coffee, but in

229

the main, that was about all the entertainment we had.

With the children and going to college trying to finish my degree, I wasn't able to work, but I did have access to a good library at Berea College. That kept me in quality reading material.

On campus, the Phelps-Stokes Chapel occasionally presented a movie shown on a screen pulled down from above the stage. Holiday presentations there were always a delight, and when the symphony came to Berea from Louisville, I took my children. On one occasion we took our seats in the first row of the balcony, and it's a wonder that Alex didn't topple head over the rail and fall into the seats below. I could not keep him in his seat with such a good view of the orchestra at the railing. It was quite a performance by both.

The first home that Nicholas came to was our High Street house. But after I moved back home to North Carolina with him just a toddler, he had little association with his father or Berea. Just a decade later Taylor died, so Nick grew up during that time with his grandfather and older brothers as father-figures. A year or so after Taylor's death, our old friend from the truck driving days, Jacob Michael, and I became reacquainted and subsequently married. For the next thirty years or so, he was the man of the house, and Michael became the family name by marriage. Nicholas knew him more as Dad than his real father but kept his actual name.

Jacob was a kindly sort of man who had married once while in England during a stint in the service. That union didn't work out, and he ended up making a career out of the Air Force rising up the ranks to be a highly qualified Sergeant.

He was one of several brothers from a prominent land-holding, farming family in the Davidson County area of North Carolina. With no children of his own, he took up the role of father for Nick, and did well.

We tended to our gardens in both counties and lived in the same little house that Daddy had built years ago as a share-cropper's residence from the remains of

Jacob, youngest of the Michael boys, during an Air Force hitch in England.

disassembled Burch station structures. This little, metal roofed house served us well, as it did four of my children during goodly portions of their growing up years. And it continues to keep me both warm and dry. I still do a little gardening out back, not like we used to, just some leafy greens and onions in the spring, beans and things during summer, turnips and greens and apples in the fall, and staying warm in winter.

All this is far afield from High Street and Berea College, but it's all connected through my memories and my children.

Jacob was quite a gardener, another giant turnip!

My oils, pastels, drawings and sketches hang on walls here and there. This alter work, one among other large oils for churches, has been displayed in the Salem Fork Christian Church for decades.

Our River Yadkin

Way up in Watauga County,
    mountain springs feed,
        a fast little stream;
    flowing southeast toward Lenoir.
Then bending northeast,
    the river winds the Brushies,
        in Wilkes and wanders some;
    reined in by the dam of Scott Reservoir.
Waters released go rushing,
    past Roaring River and Ronda,
        by Jonesville high on bluffs;
    facing Elkin there on t'other side.
The river spreads wider here,
    bridged by a high span,
        where floods once rampaged;
    waters flow on now rarely to rise.
Easterly between Surry and Yadkin,
    collecting Mitchell waters at Burch,
        more, too, then to Bailie Bottoms;
    by Pilot Mountain and Saura land.
Turned southward in the big bend,
    from the flat of Donnaha,
        muddy waters flow wide and still;
    by distant East Bend once so grand.
Calm by Shallowford, Salisbury's Trading Ford,
    Then, reined in once again,
        by High Rock Dam and more;
    our river Yadkin becomes the Pee Dee.
A quiet river once home to peoples of the woods,
    flows on through time as it should,
        the Yadkin name lost but to few,
    meanders its way on to the sea.

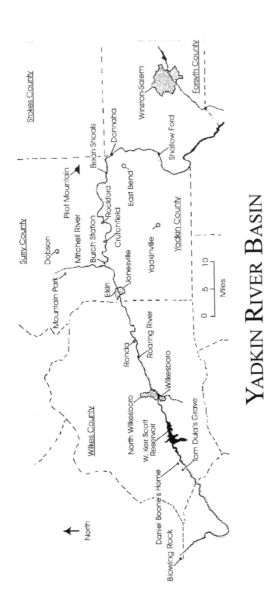

YADKIN RIVER BASIN

234

O Technology

It has been a while since I started this writing, and many old photos have reminded me of people and places long forgotten. One picture - the well at my old home - started a chain reaction.

Water, one bucket a winding, was toted up a flight of steps, beyond a screen door, across a porch, and into the kitchen, B. E. (Before Electricity).

Likewise, wood by the armloads was brought to fire the Majestic range. Only then could cooking begin.

Mama and me by the well between our house and the barn c. 1925

235

The miracle of push-button living came with REA in the Forties. Today I had an oven fire - the bottom unit flamed out. So I called Duke Power, phones are commonplace now. Got "Press One, Press two..." the modern sorter system. "Appliance Service" gave me a phone number to call, and a living person in Norfolk, Virginia, answered and told me that a service man would be available next Tuesday.

And it came to pass. My ten year old range got a transplant, all by the methods of technology that has connected the small but ever so wondrous world of my childhood with the world at large.

Once, a long time ago, I played a Harmonium at church, pedaling furiously. Now a nice electric organ/piano duo at the Salem Fork Christian Church effortlessly "heists the tune." When I reached seventy-five, a young musician took over my job behind the potted plant.

The Interstate highway by quiet Salem Fork funnels traffic along at a furious pace. Cars are everywhere in this age of metal. When my grandson, Wesley, finished medical school, I flew - FLEW- to Memphis for his graduation. And to fulfill a life-long want, I boarded the Delta Queen at its Memphis dock and landed five days later in New Orleans. Imagine that! The mood was just right: a wooden steamboat, seventy-five years old, for an Octogenarian. And they let me play the steam Calliope; my cup runneth over.

This year I turn eighty... don't ask me HOW? I just lived and it happened.